More praise for *The Wounded Male*

"I found *The Wounded Male* to be not only a sterling example of vulnerability with strength, but realistically and pragmatically helpful with concrete suggestions on journaling and establishing/maintaining a men's group—indispensable processes of recovery. . . . One of, if not *the*, most straightforward, sensitive, intelligent, helpful and succinct books in the men's movement."

> —Anthony S. Jones, Ph.D.
> Founder, The National Association of
> Adult Children of Dysfunctional Families

"Steven Farmer gives a valuable 'down-to-earth' description of men's recovery in *The Wounded Male*. . . . I highly recommend this book for men who want practical tools for responding to their calling through the male wound."

> —Kip Flock, L.C.S.W.
> Clinical Director
> John Bradshaw Center at Ingleside Hospital

"It is clearly evident that Steven Farmer is a person of deep empathy and has participated in the healing of his own wounds and, most important, in his talk and his walk is providing healing for others. Thank you Steven."

> —George Emery
> The Emissary Foundation

"With *The Wounded Male*, Steven Farmer takes us down to the pain and out again into the light."

> —Jed Diamond
> Author of *Inside Out: Becoming My Own Man*

"*The Wounded Male* is an excellent book about men. I highly recommend it."

> —John C. Friel, Ph.D.
> Director, Lifeworks Clinic

"A straightforward, no-nonsense [...] men's issues. I liked it a lot. It's easy to understand a[...]

> —Marvin Alle[...]
> Director of [...]

D1115944

THE
WOUNDED MALE

Steven Farmer

BALLANTINE BOOKS • NEW YORK

Library of Congress Catalog Card Number: 92-90116
ISBN: 0-345-37432-0

Cover design by Dale Fiorillo
Cover photograph by H. Pelletier—Superstock
Text design by Holly Johnson

Manufactured in the United States of America

First Ballantine Books Edition: August 1992

10 9 8 7 6 5 4 3 2 1

To Richard, Bruce, Paul, and Ramos,
men who have taught me how to love the earth and sky

Contents

List of Exercises

Acknowledgments

I want to acknowledge the men from my men's groups for their inspiration and support, Alan Garner for his tireless coaching, Pat Peret for her loving encouragement, and Janice Gallagher for her superlative editorial assistance.

Preface

Many of us men are already on a healing journey; many more of us are curious or interested but uncertain how to go about it. I wrote this book *for* you and *to* you, no matter where you are in the healing of your own wounds.

My path started a few years ago when I recognized some of the traumatic experiences I'd had both as a child and as a man and realized that I had never grieved these experiences, never fully felt the pain and anguish that a person is *supposed* to feel when he is wounded. I also realized that somewhere along the way I had shut off my feelings and was becoming dead inside, feeling increasingly distant and remote from others. I had hit a point where I was emotionally and spiritually bankrupt, where I had bottomed out and could no longer continue my self-destructive denial. By my remoteness and my absence I was hurting people around me, especially those whom I loved the most.

Through my own awakening process it became apparent that there were some ways in which I was wounded specifically because of my gender—because I was male—and that this was true for most other men. For example, the absent father has had profound implications for both boys and girls, but as boys we faced a particular dilemma as sons in trying to find out how to be a man without a man's being available to teach us. As a gender we men have learned to be astoundingly numb to our emotions as a consequence of our woundedness.

The past few years have seen an enthusiastic and growing

interest and concern in men's issues, as more and more men came to the forefront with their tales of woundedness, tales that had up to this time been pushed aside in favor of a relentless pursuit of success and a dogmatic attachment to isolation. Through such inspirational leaders as Robert Bly, Michael Meade, John Lee, Sam Keen, and a few others, we began to come together as men and discover a deeper and fuller meaning to being a man. In order to do so, what was required has been nothing less than a massive cleansing of the wound, sometimes reopening old scars in order that they properly heal. It isn't so much that there's a men's movement, which implies political and social action to right some wrongs, but that there is something powerful moving *in* men and *between* men, an emotional and spiritual surge of loving and powerful male energy that is coming to life and having an effect on all who come into contact with it.

Through this massive male awakening a few excellent books have come along to address our concerns, notably *Flying Boy*, *Iron John*, and *Fire In the Belly*, to name a few. Until now, however, there has been no practical guidebook. That was my purpose in writing this book—to offer some solid guidelines for your journey, as well as some examples of what other men, including myself, have gone through in our own healing process. It is written from the perspective of a heterosexual, Caucasian male, yet I'm sure that if you don't fit that particular category, you will still find a great deal that you can relate to in this book.

Although this is written to men and for men, if you are a woman I hope you will find *The Wounded Male* enlightening. Ultimately, the journey is something we have to do by trial and error and by trusting our own inner guidance, yet I'm sure there will be times when this book will come in handy.

The exercises presented throughout the book should be particularly helpful. Each one is designed to help you relate through your own personal experience to the ideas presented in the text. Please see the table of contents for a complete list of the exercises—or just read on.

I would like to encourage you to use a journal along with this book to record your thoughts and feelings while you are on this healing journey. Specifically, get in the habit of writing at least a little bit each day about your personal discoveries, observations, and experiences with the exercises. Although you may choose to let someone else read your journal, it should be written for you and you alone.

If it is at all possible, try working with this book with a man friend. This way, the two of you can share with each other your struggles and your insights as you work through the various sections. It may be the start of what could eventually become a men's support group. In the last chapter you will find detailed information on how to start your own support group.

Throughout, you will find stories based on true life examples from men I have known. Although names and identifying details have been changed, the essential point of the stories remains the same. The only exceptions are the vignettes from my life, which remain considerably accurate despite the name changes.

I also invite you to write me about how you are healing your woundedness. I will not be able to write back, but if you write, I promise I will read your letter. Send any correspondence to: Steven Farmer, P.O. Box 10052, Newport Beach, California, 92658.

Best of all to you in your healing.

1

"I Can Handle It"

THE WALKING WOUNDED

Mike presents a public image that is all too common. The picture of success—good-looking, financially secure, with a beautiful wife, two children, and an established career in management in which he has climbed the corporate ladder—he has, by most anyone's definition, "made it." Why then is he so miserable? Why then has he decided to separate from his wife after eighteen years of marriage? And why then does he carry so much tension coiled up in his body? "I'm not sure of all the 'whys,' " he replied, "but I do know something isn't right with my life. Now that I'm living on my own I feel free of the day-to-day obligations of family life. But I really miss my wife and kids. I'm totally consumed with work. I keep getting these massive headaches. I'm having trouble sleeping at night. I'm handling it okay, I guess, but I'm getting tired of living like this."

Mike has learned to handle a lot in his lifetime. Though you wouldn't necessarily guess it from his outward appearance, he is deeply wounded. The effects of his wounds are becoming so evident in his life that he can't ignore them anymore. Yet for his friends and family he continues to play out the charade of having it all together, even though the plaster image is cracking. The pain and anguish that he had tucked away so long ago have been covered over for many years by his ambition and his competitiveness. As he has gotten older, he has used his work

1

increasingly as a means to placate his nagging self-doubts. As with many men, work was the one arena in which he could have a semblance of control and mastery, even when the rest of his life was falling apart. By throwing himself into his work, he could keep his distance from other people and thus avoid the deep, unsettled grief and pain connected with the wounds that he has accumulated through the years. Now, though, the cracks in his armor are showing up in near-debilitating physical symptoms.

The earliest wounds can be some of the most damaging. One of Mike's most prominent early memories is the fights between his mother and father. "My dad would go on a drunk and inevitably there would be a fight and he would end up beating her up. My older sister would run off to her room, so there was no one else there to help my mom but me. Once when I was about nine or ten, I went after my dad, my fists flying, when he was slapping her around. He grabbed me, picked me up, threw me into my room, and locked the door. I lay there crying, pounding my fists on the floor, listening to her screams and the sounds of my dad hitting her. I felt so helpless that day. I've hated my father ever since."

Like many of us, Mike learned to conceal his rage and his hurt over such abusive treatment behind a facade of stoic toughness and emotional inaccessibility. Buried beneath this facade are the wounds of never really knowing his father other than as a tyrant, of being cast in the role of his mother's defender/ protector, and of having no one to acknowledge his feelings, especially his hurt and his pain. Buried are the wounds of never having experienced genuine closeness with a man, of going into adulthood thinking that women are to be protected rather than related to; buried as well is the wound of the terrible distance that he feels from his own depth of feelings, from his core of being. His well-rehearsed survival tactics have led Mike today to look good on the outside, to be able to pretend that he's in control, all the while feeling terribly empty and isolated on the inside. It is only as a result of his current crisis that he has been willing to look inside himself and discover that he is much more than his outer appearance. In doing so, however, he is also discovering the untended suffering of all the wounds that came before.

Most of us men have been carrying deep wounds, wounds that have never completely healed. When these wounds remain unhealed we carry their lasting pain, even though we hide it behind supposedly male bravado. These wounds have been buried so deeply that we've spent the majority of our lives being only faintly aware—if we are aware at all—of how they have hurt us, our relationships, and our work. While they may not have crippled us totally, these lingering wounds have resulted in unresolved pain, blunted emotions, and inaccessibility, characteristics that are so common among men we assume they're part and parcel of what it is to be male.

We have untreated wounds from childhood and adulthood. From childhood come the immensely harmful wounds of a father who was absent or remote and a mother who was an overly strong presence. The wounds of physical or emotional battering from either parent leave their scars, as well as the confusion and secret pain of sexual abuse. We have assumed our forefathers' spiritual wounds, the wounds of losing touch with the earth and the seasons of nature. All the ungrieved and unacknowledged disappointments, hurts, and losses throughout our lives are wounds, as well as the shame that stifles the expression of our natural selves. There are the wounds that come from having to be warriors in the barbaric ritual of war, as well as the ones that come from having to continually perform and achieve, which is supposed to yield some strange quotient of worthiness. Then there is the wound that comes from the contrast between how we see ourselves and the sense that we are meant to be more than we are; that we are not meant to be mere automatons serving the false gods of corporation or state, but alive, awake, living beings. We are meant to be men in the truest sense of the word.

We are the walking wounded. This tendency to hide our pain, our vulnerability, and in many instances our anger from ourselves and from the world around us is a tragic misuse of our life energy. It often leads us to acting out some caricature of how we think we are supposed to be as men, a particular image that becomes increasingly honed as we age. Like Mike, we learn very early on to present a picture of "I have it together—I can handle it" to those around us. Because those men around us are usually living out a similar pretense, they readily accept this image. It becomes a game of "I'll buy your act if you buy mine."

Although being wounded is not unique to men—many women can readily identify with some of the wounds that have been and will be described—the implications of certain injuries, such as the absence of father, have had a devastatingly profound impact on our core identity as men. In addition, what is particular to men are the characteristic ways we have adjusted to our wounds. We have learned to isolate ourselves behind the guise of being "rugged individualists," to forbid ourselves our needs and our vulnerability, to mask our emotions, and slowly to extinguish our vitality and enthusiasm, all for the sake of hiding the degree to which we are wounded.

The Wounded Boy

A man can be wounded at any time during his life, but the injuries he experiences during childhood are the ones that have the most lasting impact and the most far-reaching consequences. These are the wounds from physical or verbal battering, from sexual abuse, or from the absence of any genuine closeness with father or mother. These are the wounds from the hundreds, perhaps thousands of times a little boy's heart ached for real love, and love was not there.

What's tragic is not only that the child has been victimized by the misuse of parental power and authority, but that this hurt little boy then conceals his feelings, his needs, and his spirit. This profoundly injured little boy remains trapped deep inside us as we become men.

"I remember one day, as my father was whipping me with a belt, I decided to turn off my feelings, to not cry," George said. "That was to let my father know that his beatings weren't bothering me. After that, whenever I did slip and show any pain I'd get really mad at myself, because then he knew that he had gotten to me.

"My mother slapped me sometimes and was constantly putting me down, but she didn't beat me. Whenever she wanted the dirty work done she'd sic my dad on me. It was the old routine of 'just wait until your father gets home.' There were many times when I'd be waiting all day, terrified, and sure enough, when he got home he'd start in on me. I really hated her for the way she'd set my dad against me."

George betrays this earlier mistreatment through his body language. When he looks around, his eyes do all the looking; his head, rigidly fixed to his short, barrel-chested torso, barely moves. It seems that at the first sign of danger he will pull his head down, like a turtle, into his shell. His body is armored, shielding against any possible assault. He looks as if he not only would not let anything in, but that he wouldn't let anything out. This stiff way of carrying his body became necessary when he was a vulnerable little boy.

It's important to respect and appreciate just how tender and needy this little human being is who comes into the world. He must rely totally on the adults around him to care for him, to love him, to provide him with all the essentials to support his life and welfare. For the first several years of his life he is utterly dependent on these adults for his very survival. When nurturing, genuine, healthy relationships with parents are lacking, and in their place are beatings, shame, neglect, humiliation, or abandonment, then—like George—a boy has to deny certain innate qualities of his being. He must deny and repress his feelings, desires, needs, spontaneity, and vitality.

For instance, it is the most natural thing in the world for a child to cry when he is hurt, yet how many of us have heard that familiar parental refrain, "You'd better stop your crying or I'll give you something to cry about!" Such a response allows the child no choice other than to sublimate his hurt and his pain, to swallow his sobs. Otherwise, he faces further punishment and shame from someone several times his size. And if a giant tells you to shut up, you shut up! With enough practice at stifling his feelings, a boy gets very good at it—in fact, so good that he may learn not to feel at all.

As a little boy, I instinctively knew that it was dangerous to be open and to feel my emotions. I learned to shut down my feelings and my passion from as far back as I can recall. In my family, it was too scary, too threatening, to remain fully awake and alive. Bouts of parental tension and fighting were followed by long periods of calm. Yet even these quieter times were suspect, filled with the ominously reliable prospect of the next fracas. This ongoing drama usually centered around my father's drinking, yet it was a play that the whole family enacted. My mother's part would be to shout and scream a lot, either at my dad or my older brother, and my older brother's role was to be the focus for much of the tension between my parents by frequently getting into trouble, thereby provoking a new round of fights.

I would often wait with anticipation for my father to come home after his long day driving a bulldozer. I really looked forward to his arrival. There was something quite special and attractive about having this man as my father, since he drove huge machines that could move the earth. He was a big strong man. I looked up to him; against his and my mother's wishes, I secretly longed to be like him. My mother would have had me be a doctor, probably so I could care for her ailments, while my father would simply have had me go to college and not have to do such backbreaking work as driving a machine.

The clock would tick past the expected time of arrival. Four o'clock. Quarter past. Four-thirty. Five o'clock. All this time my mother would be working herself into a fret, expressing certainty that he was "down at the Sixteenth Avenue bar, getting drunk again," and she was invariably right. The tension mounted. My dad would walk in, wobbly, reeling from all the beers he had drunk, and *blam!* She would start in right away. "Di-i-ick!" The memory of the way she would shout his name still sends shivers down my spine.

I would be sitting on the couch in the living room, usually

watching TV, doing my best not to show the intense fear that I was feeling, hoping that my pounding heart would not betray me. My older brother and sister, being wise to this scene, had by now gone to their rooms or else had already made other arrangements so that they would not have to witness this inevitable clash. I felt very alone and unprotected, with a maelstrom of chaotic energy surrounding me, sucking me into its depths.

I wanted to cry out, to yell at them both, "Stop!" I yearned for someone to rescue me from this all-too-familiar drama, someone to be there, someone to make my fear go away. I felt torn between the need to be a "brave little man" and tough it out, and my desire to shriek to the world about my fear and desperation. I wanted to hurt my father, to shake him to his senses, while at the same time I wanted to scream at my mother to leave him alone, to let him just come home and quietly go to sleep.

The route I usually chose—as if there was truly any other choice—was to quietly slip away into my room. There I would undress for bed, stopping every so often so that I could listen closely to the shouting that was going on a few feet away outside my bedroom door. If there was a pause, I would hold my breath in order to hear what would come next. Sometimes it was just a lull in the fighting, sometimes they had gone to their respective corners in an uneasy truce, and other times I would hear the grunts and groans that indicated the fights had become physical. I was horrified, but had to stay in my room because I didn't want to come out and witness exactly what was taking place. There were many nights when I cried myself to sleep, not certain what I would wake up to the next day.

It's difficult for most of us men truly to know the terror and pain a child can experience until we remember, relive, and feel anew our own repressed childhood traumas. It is not a case of digging into the past, as if that were its own end, or simply of coming up with horror stories from childhood. Instead, as we recall the pain and anguish of boyhood wounds, we can develop a greater empathy for ourselves and others, thereby allowing the healing process to begin. Whether it is the terror of being physically beaten by someone many times our size, being sexually abused by an adult charged with our care, the tyranny of hateful words, or the tremendous fear and emptiness that come from being a little boy and having no adult there to care for you, it is a private hell that must be endured through tremendous cost to a young boy's spirit.

Add to this mix the common expectation that little boys in particular are not expected to cry, to show any vulnerable feelings. There is ongoing teasing and shaming to discourage boys from honest emotional expression. Boys who do cry face the risk of being called a sissy or a crybaby. Although it's fine for little girls to be called "daddy's girl," it's humiliating for a boy to be called a "momma's boy," another shaming name that was thrown at you if you cried or showed the need for any love or comfort. Boys are expected early in life to learn to control their feelings and not to make a fuss, to behave like "little men" once they have passed the age of six or seven—in other words, to be controlled, unfeeling, and tough. How sad it is that we as a culture have expected this of little boys!

Whatever the specific scenario, when a child is abused by an adult, has to witness an adult out of control, or is parented by an adult who is physically or emotionally absent, a deep wound results, one that scars the psyche and leaves considerable unresolved pain until a man begins his recovery and healing.

Adding Insult To Injury

The traumas of childhood are not alone in being injurious. Every boy will face pain and disillusionment, will at times have to suffer, whether alone or in the company of peers or parents. There will be injuries from falling off his bicycle, from being chosen last for the soccer team, from receiving an unexpectedly low grade in a class, from being taunted by a classmate.

It's not just the injury itself that leaves scars, however; it's the manner in which the adults around the child react to this injury. It isn't necessary that an adult feel sorry for the boy, but the healthiest response that an adult can make to a child who has been wounded is, first and foremost, to acknowledge the child's feelings. This requires that the adult be present, be available, and have an empathy that reaches in and touches the child exactly where he is emotionally. For most of us, neither mother nor father was able to provide this sort of response in our lives. In fact, often one or both parents contributed to the child's suffering by adding further hurt to the existing trauma.

When I was about nine years old, my mother decided she wanted me to try out for baseball. My brother did his best to encourage me, but since I had played very little baseball, his efforts were futile. I was not feeling very open to encouragement, to say the least. I was scared to death of trying out. Nonetheless, the next morning I was there, signed up to be on a team where I knew no one, feeling totally inept and finding nowhere to hide. My mother, who was excited about the prospect of her youngest son playing America's favorite pastime, had sent me to the first practice with a brand-new, never-been-used baseball glove with RAWLINGS splashed across the huge leather palm.

Practice proceeded as I imagine most Little League practices do. Catching the ball was one of the first drills. It didn't take long for the coach to realize that asking me to catch a baseball was like asking someone who has never been fishing to bait the hook and set the fishing line. Throwing my hands into the air, palms up, closing my eyes, and ducking my head was not the most efficient way to catch a ball, but that's the best I knew how to do. The coach didn't say much; he didn't have to.

Batting practice was more of the same. I swung at that ball like a woodsman chopping down a tree. At least with a tree, I'd have stood a chance of hitting something. Not so with a nine-year-old boy who'd never held a bat in his life aiming at a little ball about three inches in diameter. After a few swings that mainly fanned the air and prompted impatient, hands-on-the-hips looks from the outfielders, I was relegated to right field.

Right field is where they typically banish the boys who don't know how to catch. Needless to say, the coach was not impressed.

At the end of practice, he gathered us all around and talked about the practices to come. I began to feel even a little excitement at the prospect of playing baseball. Then—horror of horrors—just as the rest of the guys started dispersing, he looked at me and told me he wanted to talk with me. Once we were alone, he suggested that it might be better if I waited until next year to play. Feeling as though I'd taken a kick in the guts, I didn't even hear any more of what he said after that. All I could hear was my inner voice saying, "I'm being kicked off the team. I'm being kicked off the team." My face started swelling with stifled tears. There was a hot lump in my throat as I swallowed my intense disappointment. I felt totally humiliated, embarrassed, and ashamed, but I was not about to show it to anyone.

The coach stopped in midsentence as he was tactfully choosing his words of dismissal—I think he caught the look on my face—and said, "New glove, eh?" I looked down at this grotesque monstrosity affixed to my hand and nodded affirmation. He looked a bit embarrassed himself, as if he suddenly realized that I was on the verge of tears. He then went on, "Well, tell you what. Come on back tomorrow and we'll see what we can do." But it was too late. He had already proclaimed my demise. It's as if both he and I knew that I wouldn't be back but had to act out this necessary charade for the sake of avoiding unpleasant feelings of grief and embarrassment. What would I tell my mom? What would my brother say? How could I ever face them after this? Could we take the glove back?

I walked over to where my mother was going to pick me up and sat there stunned, holding on to my anger and disappointment, yet also feeling a curious sense of relief. All I could do was stare at the stupid glove. When my mother arrived and I haltingly told her what had happened, she confirmed my worst nightmare. "I'll talk with that damn coach," she said. "I can't believe he'd do that. After I just bought you that glove they'd better let you play on the team." Despite my feeble protests, she insisted that I return the next day, vowing that she would "tell that coach a thing or two."

While in any rational sense my being rejected from the baseball team was certainly not the end of the world, even now as I write these words I can feel some of the sadness, humiliation, and anger that I experienced at the time. I can even intellectually justify what happened, understand it, or apply some sort of spiritual brainwashing such as "It was meant to be." But while these things may contain some truth, I cannot deny the *fact* that at the time I felt absolutely miserable. Even today I can tap into those feelings of shame and humiliation.

So it is not only the wounds of defeat or of other hurtful experiences that a child can have. Injury is compounded and insult is added if the adult rebukes the child, shames him, tells him his feelings are wrong, or suggests that he should act like a "little man" when in fact what the boy needs is genuine parental empathy, a sincere appreciation and acknowledgment of what he is feeling. In some instances his internal pain is magnified by the total absence of a parental figure, leaving him to "handle" his feelings himself. In any of these situations, a boy learns to turn off, to minimize his genuine suffering, to repress his natural inclination to experience and express his hurt and his anger. With my mother's response to my Little League disaster, for example, my embarrassment cut deeply into my soul. I wouldn't dare cry or honestly show my fear because I was even more afraid that she would tease me or tell my dad or brother, who would both think I was a real wimp.

My mother was true to her word. She did talk to the coach, and I did return the next day. But in my silently defiant way, I knew that I was done with baseball. I played a little bit more in right field, showed up at bat once in a while, but my spirit was gone. This lasted for about a week before I began coming up with excuses for missing practices and eventually stopped going altogether. I was glad to put the whole experience behind me. Throughout it all I knew that I would never reveal to anyone all of the confusing feelings that were churning inside me;

my ongoing training as a young boy told me it wasn't okay to express any of these feelings, that it was better if I just learned to "take it and fake it."

LET'S PRETEND

To deny our woundedness has sadly become the norm for manhood. This is a result of childhood training coming from the family and, more broadly, from the culture that has given all of us—men and women—a very distorted notion of what manhood is all about. From this training we have learned a certain code of behavior that causes us to hide away our natural expressiveness and instead come up with a way of acting "normal." Life becomes a game of "Let's Pretend" wherein you continually try to get other people to buy your image but hide from most—perhaps even all—people your true self. Most of the other men you meet will also be trying to sell you their image, whether they are aware of it or not, since they, too, are playing Let's Pretend. Then, to compound our denial, we pretend that we're not pretending!

For the majority of us, pretending started very early. The image or role you assumed was shaped from childhood but was refined as you grew into manhood. You may have taken on the role of the perfectionist, the caretaker, the superhero, the invisible one, the macho man, the rebel, the nice guy, or any combination of these. Over time this role became a rigid and deciding factor in the way in which you related to your world, stifling a broader range of experience and expressiveness, but most of all offering a convenient, well-rehearsed way to stay safe and hide from the world.

Sam had hidden out from people in many ways throughout his life. He is easygoing and quick to smile, yet his eyes dart away if eye contact lasts longer than a few seconds. His thin frame looks as if it were bound tightly with wire. When he jams his hands into his denims his long arms hunch his shoulders up close to his ears in an awkward attempt to look casual.

He says: "I have a hard time being around most people. I don't have any close friends, although I do have a few of what you would call acquaintances. I've only had one girl friend in my thirty years, and even though we broke up over five years ago, I still miss her a lot. I've been working in the same job for quite a few years now, and haven't once gotten a promotion. When I finally got up the nerve to ask them about a management position, I got the big stall. My boss said he'd get back to me, and I haven't heard from him since. That was over two months ago."

Sam feels distant not only from others but also from himself. "I know I shut down a long time ago but I'm not sure when. I don't remember a lot of my past, but I do remember when my dad left. He would almost always play with me at least a little while when he first came home. He took these long trips—he was a truck driver—and so I wouldn't see him for days at a time, but when he did come home it was a big deal for both my mom and me. One day he just didn't come home. That was it. He was supposed to show up and he didn't. I was waiting up for him—it was kind of late—so my mom put me to bed, and he still wasn't there the next day. I cried and cried— that was probably the last time I can remember really crying— but he had just disappeared. My mom never explained it to me. I guess she was caught up in her own feelings. I wasn't allowed to talk about him after that. Every time I brought his name up she'd either get angry or start crying, so I learned pretty quickly not to talk about him. I looked him up a few years ago and called him but he never returned my call. I guess he still doesn't want anything to do with me."

Sam's role was to be as invisible as possible to the world, so he wouldn't stir things up or create any problems. He buried the pain of his loss and learned to hide behind his shyness, acting out a role of always being nice and accommodating, staying as much out of the way of others as possible. This role served its purpose when he was growing up, but now it just keeps him isolated and lonely. Like most of us he learned to adjust in the best possible way to his dysfunctional family, but now the behavior pattern that he learned so well as a young boy rigidly constricts him as a man. His conditioning keeps him shy and unhappy, emotionally numb and afraid to be with people.

Behind our individual roles, our personal games of Let's Pretend, we carry the worn baggage of our woundedness. We may be only vaguely aware of the pain, or we may be acutely sensitive to it. When we're only vaguely aware of it, we try to avoid feeling it, especially by keeping busy, even though we still may experience a fleeting sense of emptiness or loneliness. When we are sensitive to it, we may either try to tough it out, medicate it, isolate ourselves even more, act as if nothing is troubling us, or, as more men are willing to do these days, make some attempts to feel it and work with it. However, by walking around and pretending our pain isn't there by trying to shove it away, we only delay the inevitable. Some day we will have to reconcile our woundedness; otherwise we continue to hurt ourselves and others. Avoiding our feelings is always a very temporary measure. By doing so we may temporarily avoid pain but we also avoid any deeper feelings of love and joy.

Jerry, like so many others, prides himself on his ability to stay calm, cool, and collected even in the most dire of circumstances. While this is an admirable quality in a crisis, Jerry has difficulty dropping this trait at other times when it's obviously not needed. His rigidly rational approach to situations, such as those involving his wife, Sheila, has sometimes led to even bigger upsets.

After a dispute over whether or not to invest money in a particular real estate deal, Sheila got very angry with him. For the first time in their seven-year relationship, she threatened to divorce him. Taken aback, Jerry withdrew from her, obviously hurt but not knowing what to say. "If she wants to divorce me, then she can," Jerry said in a controlled, subdued voice, belying his fear and his hurt. "She's being totally irrational. I just don't want to play that way." When challenged as to his hurt and angry feelings, Jerry said, "I don't care to feel those kinds of feelings. Why suffer when you don't have to? I'd just as soon not be married than to have to feel those kinds of feelings."

Covering The Pain

Jerry is willing to maintain his outward show of strength and togetherness at the potential cost of his relationship. Like Jerry, many of us men have continued to "handle" our lives, our relationships, and especially our feelings—at the cost of a lot of hurt and pain to ourselves and others. The emotional numbing learned in childhood does not make the pain go away completely, but it does hold it down and cover it over, often keeping it from conscious awareness. When we cover our pain, we cover *all* of our feelings. With enough practice we get very good at disguising our inner turmoil; once we reach adulthood, there is plenty of reinforcement for us as men to continue to rein our feelings in. Unfortunately, avoiding feelings in this way leads to depression. Usually a man doesn't know he's depressed because it's his "normal" state and, furthermore, society encourages this Marlboro Man approach to feeling. We only know how depressed we are after we come out of the depression and start feeling. If you are used to black-and-white television, you simply assume that there is no other kind. When you see your first program in full living color, then you realize the limitations of the black-and-white model.

To cover your woundedness and depression and cope with the underlying feelings that get harder to suppress as you get older, you may find yourself using alcohol, food, work, television, sex, or something similar to ease the pain. It may develop that you are using either the substance—such as alcohol—or the activity—such as work—addictively, as a way of escaping from feelings that you don't know how to deal with. At the same time, whatever is used addictively will allow you to feel *something*. For example, alcohol numbs the sensations while at the same time releasing inhibitions. Often someone who otherwise holds his feelings in may be able to cry or laugh much more easily after one or two drinks. Sex, when used in an addictive way, can provide stimulation and release, yet at the same time may serve to cover and avoid other feelings, such as fear or sadness. Work when performed addictively can be an activity that lets you feel good about yourself because you are being productive and achieving, while at the same time helping you avoid intimacy or any personal dealings with other people.

Although the addictive use of drugs and alcohol is the most destructive, whatever you use will strangle the vitality out of you over a period of time, leaving you repressed and numb to your feelings. When you're addicted, you never touch your depression, never work with it. Your feelings remain deadened, but are instead toyed with and artificially stimulated by the substance or the activity to which you are addicted. And to heal the wounds you must begin honestly to feel once again, and to grieve.

The point is that these addictive behaviors keep us numb to our underlying grief and anguish. I look back at my life and am sometimes amazed at how I ever survived this long. At various times I've used alcohol, marijuana, cocaine, and psychedelics addictively. I've used sex, relationships, eating, and cigarettes addictively. I'm forty-three years old, and well over half my adult life (and probably most of my childhood) I was clinically depressed and didn't know it. I seriously considered suicide at least three times, and there were two occasions when I almost inadvertently killed myself with an overdose of cocaine. I've been through two marriages and two divorces, both of them to very good women. I've been through many relationships, most of them ending because I didn't know what I wanted and didn't know how to be intimate beyond a certain point. Sex was the pivotal way that I could be close to a woman; I didn't know what it meant to be just friends. And up until the last few years I've never had a close friendship with a man, one in which we could share our innermost feelings.

I'm sure that any man reading this can easily recognize and relate to the isolation and loneliness that I have felt. I learned to cover this up not only with my addictive behavior, but with my "act." I was one of those shy men who did his best not to make waves, to impress everyone with how "nice" I was. My public persona became more and more split from my private behavior: practicing an open marriage with my first wife that was open only in its sexual practices but not in its emotional and spiritual sharing, doing drugs surreptitiously while I was counseling others, acting as if I were faithful in my second marriage while having affairs. The incongruity of my public self and my private self, and the no-win direction I was heading in came painfully into focus during my second divorce. I realized then how much I had been living a lie, and how much I had hurt myself and others by doing so.

For one of the few times in my life, I let myself grieve, to feel the immense sadness and hurt, the massive pain of not only the wounds of the divorce, but of all the wounds I had accumulated up to that point. Denial no longer worked. Addictions no longer worked. At that point I could no longer avoid what I was feeling.

It really hit me shortly after my second wife, Susan, and I separated. I had just spent the day with my older daughter, Nicole, who was four years old at the time. We had a wonderful time together, and I was thrilled to have been with her. Then it came time to return her to her mother. As I was driving her there and we got to the final few blocks, I began to cry. Up to that time, Nicole had never seen tears in my eyes. I told her I was feeling very sad, that I didn't know how to deal with what was going on, and that I didn't like having to leave her after having such a great time with her. She kept to herself and said nothing, but she looked very frightened.

When we arrived at our destination I composed myself—God forbid I should let Susan see me this vulnerable!—and rather quickly said my good-byes and drove away. Once again the tears started, but as they did I noticed a check that I had neglected to give to Susan. So after driving about two blocks I wiped my tears and headed back. When I pulled up this time, Nicole was in her mother's arms, crying wildly, screaming out her own pain. I could barely walk as I got out of my car and gave the check to Susan. I held Nicole for a few moments, desperately trying to contain my own tears, aching on the inside. After a bit, Nicole went once again to her mother and I got in my car and drove away a second time.

I screamed and shouted in my car all the way home, touching a core of grief that I hadn't known existed inside me. I kept picturing my little Nicole, how she had held back her tears in the car, and how she had been sobbing uncontrollably in her mother's arms. I felt guilty and ashamed. But more than this, I reached into a reservoir of pain and suffering and opened the gates. I don't remember the drive home, but when I did get home, I threw myself on the stairs and started pounding and cursing. I cried and raged for the next two hours, whereas up until then I had probably spent no more than a couple of minutes in my sadness and tears. Such was my introduction to healing my wounds.

Through the process of healing that was instigated by the divorce, it became obvious that I was doing something wrong. I had sired two beautiful children, and it became increasingly clear to me that I did not want to pass along to them my neurotic and self-destructive patterns of behavior. I wanted them to have a real father and, unlike me, to really know their father. Yet how could I let them know me if *I* didn't know me?

Thus in 1984 a journey of awakening began, at times in earnest, at times reluctantly. The culmination of this journey—at least so far—is this book.

A HEALING JOURNEY

Healing your woundedness always starts with first admitting to yourself that you are wounded. This in itself takes a lot of courage, but it opens the way for the journey of recovery and healing. This journey is probably one of the most challenging ones you will ever take, because the darkest parts of you must come into the light. Yet it is also one of the most exciting and rewarding journeys, because it is the journey of awakening to a deeper sense of your maleness through your healing.

It is critical that you involve others in your journey, especially other men, for friendship, validation, and support. It's also important that you take some risks and be vulnerable with others. Being vulnerable means that you are risking further injury. The truth is that it may happen. Still, by staying open and finding support, you are much more prepared to experience any feelings associated with injury. It was not safe to be vulnerable in childhood, but you can make it safe now.

There's also a certain toughness, a resolve that is part of being a man, and I like it. This trait doesn't need to be separate from being vulnerable; the two qualities can comfortably coexist. I personally would like to be in touch with both sides, my vulnerability and my toughness, at any one time, calling upon the one that is most needed in any given situation. Perhaps a new ideal for a man is to be a vulnerable warrior, always in touch with both his strength and his tenderness.

In this book I will cover the origins of your wounds and show you some ways to identify your woundedness. Throughout the chapters there are exercises that will contribute to your healing of those wounds. You'll discover ways to come to terms with your childhood injuries; heal the wounds from mother and father; take better care of yourself; open yourself emotionally and spiritually; deepen your friendships with other men; and develop greater intimacy in your relationships with women.

Throughout I will be presenting many anecdotes from men I have known personally and professionally who are at various stages of their healing. Names and personal identifying information have been changed. And I'll be discussing in some depth my own recovery because I think it will be useful for you to hear from someone who is on his own path of healing. I don't pretend to have all the answers, nor could I be so presumptuous as to say that I know what's right for you. You will find your own answers; my hope is that this book will raise important questions and give you some direction for your own process.

Your journey will be both exciting and challenging. It is obvious these days that a significant number of men are yearning to heal themselves, consciously and actively, not only from the wounds they have carried from childhood, but also from the deepest wounds that men have been carrying for centuries. Perhaps the original wound occurred when man separated himself from the current of life and instead sought to control the river rather than flow with it. Most of us sense this deep alienation from nature in our lives whether we're conscious of it or not. In our most intense grief, we mourn this separation, this original wound, and yearn for a more intimate and meaningful association with life. When you consciously acknowledge this deepest of wounds, this becomes a primary objective of any healing work you do.

So prepare yourself. Read slowly through once, then go back and do any exercises that appeal to you. Let yourself weep, feel angry, laugh, contemplate, get scared; but most of all, let yourself *feel* whatever is moving inside you. Share your journey—be willing to let others in. You no longer have to be a tough guy without needs, and you no longer have to go it alone and "handle it." With a steady commitment to truth and to life, you can be alive and fully present in whatever you do.

2

Fathers and Sons

My dad was at his most impressive when he was working, whether building our house or driving a bulldozer. Even at a very tender age, I could tell he loved his work. I admired him, usually from a distance. When he built our house I was about three or four years old, and I recall thinking at the time that I wanted to be like him.

Once when I was about eight years old he took me to work with him. I was awestruck to see that he drove huge bulldozers and other types of heavy equipment that could move the earth, but I could never reconcile this admiration I felt with the strange mixture of pride and shame he seemed to feel about his work.

The day when we drove to his work, I was scared and excited, but naturally concealing these feelings with typical boyish bravado. We drove to a job site where there was an open area surrounded by sculptured piles of dirt. Smack in the middle of it was a bulldozer, enormous, with dirt caked around the treads of tires that were at least four times my size. It looked as if it were ready to growl. My dad lifted me up to the top of the tire and climbed up after me. I was ecstatic despite my fear. He didn't say much, but I could tell he was enjoying it as much as I. Sitting in the huge black cushioned chair, he pulled me next to him, strapped us both in, turned the key, and the huge metal beast beneath us belched once or twice, then roared to life. The noise and the vibration of the machine rattled my teeth and shook my bones.

Dad unhooked the brakes and, with a deftness I could barely appreciate at the time, smoothly reached for the stick, moved it into forward gear, grabbed the steering wheel, and we were off. After we did a couple of turns, he drove toward a pile of dirt and plunged the teeth of the bucket forcefully into it. With the movement of another handle, the metal scoop steadily lifted its way up through the pile, carrying with it a mouthful of earth. He turned the machine around and drove to another smaller pile with the straight metal arms of the scraper reaching into the sky. When we reached our destination, he pushed another lever and *clunk!* The bucket dropped its load in a rush of dirt and air, sending a dust cloud up around us. No wonder he came home so caked with dirt after a day driving these machines!

After a couple more runs like this, he stopped the bulldozer, which when he did sounded more like it was purring than growling, turned to me, and said, "Do you want to try it?" Did I want to try it? I felt as if God had opened up the heavens and asked me if I wanted to take a look around. It was as if my whole life had been in preparation for this one moment. I nervously looked at my dad, but as usual did not catch his eyes.

Once I was actually in the driver's seat of this hulk of a machine, I held my breath and looked around at how high up off the ground we were. I experienced the heady realization that I was going to control a machine that could move the earth around me like it was so much powder. Consumed with anticipation, I awaited further instructions. Dad directed me to take the wheel in my hands, then proceeded to give me step-by-step directions about how to drive the machine. Finally he pressed down on the accelerator and we moved straight toward one of the piles of dirt!

As we approached and reduced our speed, he shouted at me above the roar of the machine and guided my hand to the stick that controlled the bucket. By pressing it forward, I lowered the bucket to the ground so that it was ready to gobble up some more of the loose earth. My body was tense and I was scarcely breathing as my dad steadily guided my hand forward on the stick; I watched in delight as the teeth of the bucket dug their way into another pile of dirt. I pulled the lever back and up rose the bucket, carrying its load of dirt. This was a thrill beyond compare and I was completely absorbed in it. We drove the bulldozer to another part of the landscaping job and emptied the bucket there with the three previous loads. This went on for a few minutes more. Then my dad and I parked the machine and shut it off. The residual vibrations of this great chomping beast and the ecstasy of the accomplishment filled my body and my soul.

On the drive home I had a new sense of connection with my dad. From that time on I felt I knew from firsthand experience what his work was about. I knew I had changed that day, but I wasn't sure how. I had crossed some threshold; I was very much aware that I was his son, and I knew a pride in having him for a father.

Even though I will always cherish this experience with my father, it turned out, sadly, to be the exception rather than the rule. I hoped and waited for another invitation to ride the bulldozer, but he never again included me. The memory of the time that we spent together at his job site, a time when I felt so close to him and really loved by him, contrasts sharply with so many of my other memories of him. The more typical memories are those of his being away at work a lot of the time or, when he was home, of being busy with something else; of his alcoholic blustering, and the frequent fights with my mother that followed his bouts of drinking; of his falling asleep in his favorite chair every evening, waking up only in time to go to bed; of his seeming to be a virtual stranger in our home, distant and unapproachable much of the time, monstrous and scary at others, especially when he was raging. I remember how afraid I was of him, even though he had never actually beaten me, never seriously hurt me. I never really knew my father, and he never really knew me.

THE FATHER WOUND

Most of us men bear deep wounds from our relationships with
our fathers. We did not experience having them available and
accessible as we were growing up. Whether they were disci-
plinarians or passive, uninvolved bystanders, what we each
got was only a piece of our fathers. Although we experience
other wounds from the male parent, the most damaging
wound we experienced as boys, the one that continues to
have its effects on us as men, is the wound caused by his
absence or remoteness.

Do you remember ever being held by your father? Did you
ever look your father in the eyes without feeling some veiled
terror or apprehension? Did you ever look your father in the
eyes at all? Do you recall a consistent sense of his presence, of
his willingness to be open and available to you? If he ever put
his arms around you, did you feel safe? Did you feel that he
loved you just for yourself? Did he seem to enjoy the time he
spent with you? Did he talk to you about his own pain, his
worries, his fears? Did you trust him? If the answer to any or all
of these questions is no, then you know the pain of the father
wound, the father who was remote and inaccessible.

As grown men, we suffer tremendous consequences to this
"primary" wound received from the lack of fathering during
childhood. Barry Gordon, writing on "Men and Their Fathers"
in *Men in Therapy: The Challenge of Change*, has this to say
about the typical distance sons feel from their fathers:

> [T]he impact of fathers, especially absent or distant
> ones, is enormously significant for men and can domi-
> nate how they carry themselves in their adult male
> roles. Indeed, the common emotional struggles men
> bring into therapy—high degrees of stress or anxiety,
> depression, low self-esteem, various forms of depen-
> dency or addiction, and marital dysfunction—can be
> linked in significant ways to this impact.

Not having been close to their fathers while growing up is a feeling familiar to most men. I've heard many men talk about how, even though their fathers were present in the home, they never knew them. Not only did they not know their fathers, the fathers never knew their sons. This "father hunger" that most men experienced as a child continues on into adulthood. It is a deep, often unconscious sense that the father you needed was lost along the way. You reached for him and he wasn't there. And he wasn't there again and again. On those rare occasions when you did have your father's attention, you usually were the focus of his violence or his disciplinary actions. How many of us as children have heard those few words that would strike terror in our hearts, "Just wait until your father gets home," leaving us with a notion (and rightly so) that a man's involvement in the family, if he was involved to any degree at all, was one of punishing disciplinarian.

Having an absent or remote father has other implications for a man. In order for a boy to establish his identity as a male, to learn what it means to be a man, he must give up his attachment to his first love—his mother. This in itself is a wound that a boy will have difficulty reconciling when his father is remote or altogether absent. Not only must a boy relinquish the object of his first love, but he must also form an attachment and an identification with his father. If that father is not available to guide the boy away from mother, what results is an unfinished task of seperation from mother and an incomplete relationship with a father figure. This leads to a continued dependency on women, but one that is fraught with ambivalence. As to our fathers, we are considerably in the dark.

When a boy doesn't know his father or knows him only as a tyrant, he develops a distorted, one-dimensional idea of how it is to be a man. Since our identity as men is tightly bound to how we *saw* our fathers play out their roles, and we actually *knew* very little about them, we drew conclusions about them based on very limited, frequently erroneous, information. If we saw them as distant, then we figured that distant was the way to do male. If they kept their feelings to themselves (which they most likely did), then we assumed that this was how to be a man and proceeded to emulate this. A boy whose father was a tyrant will learn to be tyrannical, either with himself or with others. Likewise a boy whose father was passive with his mother will grow up to be passive with women. Because we've been hurt by our fathers' remoteness and inaccessibility and in some cases their violence, we learned not to trust other men, to assume they would hurt us if they were given the chance. We likely saw our fathers as being self-contained and self-sufficient, so we drew the conclusion that men don't need; we proceeded to incorporate this as part of our identity as a man. Such are some of the damaging effects of the father wound.

My father's distance and emotional unavailability instigated a pattern that remained with me for much of my adult life. Other than when he had been drinking, he was quiet and passive. When he did drink, he would rage. The rage was so terrifying that I vowed I would never be like him. I would never drink the way he did, and I would never lose my temper. I knew how I did not want to be as a man, but unfortunately that gave me very little idea of how I *did* want to be. I kept my vows—sort of. I didn't drink to excess, but I did drugs. I didn't rage, as least at other people, but I did hit walls in a few apartments I lived in as a young man whenever my frustration reached an intolerable level. And in my marriage I became increasingly remote and inaccessible, even though at the time I would have looked you straight in the eyes and maintained that I wasn't at all like my dad!

There are other wounds that we receive from father, but this remoteness is the foundation for all others. We can be hurt by father through his deceit, his unkept promises, or through his physical, sexual, or emotional abuse. Jed Diamond, in an article in MAN! magazine called "Healing Male Codependency," quotes a client of his, Robert, relating a story about his father:

> "I didn't see my father a lot as a child, but I used to run to him and throw my arms around his neck when

he'd come in the door. I remember a game we played when I was maybe two or three years old. I would climb up on a chair and yell 'catch me' as I would jump into his arms, squealing with delight.

"I remember the day it happened, clear as if it was yesterday," Robert said. His expression didn't change. Only something deep in his eyes revealed his feelings. "I yelled out, 'Daddy, Daddy,' as I jumped off the kitchen chair and flew through the air with my arms outstretched. But just as I reached out to him, he turned away and I hit my head on the table as I fell to the floor. I don't remember much after that, except Dad yelling at me to be quiet as we drove to the hospital. Days later . . . Dad took me on his lap and said, "Baby boy, you have to learn—you can't trust anyone in this life, not even your own father.' "

Is this what fathers have been meant for? To teach their sons that the world is a dangerous place? That no one is to be trusted, that eventually other men will betray you, so don't trust them? When a son learns these lessons from his father he also learns to be guarded with his own feelings. Whatever your individual circumstances with your father, it's very likely that you received these kinds of messages from him. This lack of trust in other men, guardedness of feelings, and remoteness that you saw in your father and now see in yourself are the direct results of the father wound. Not only did you learn these "typical" male behaviors from your father, but for the last several generations they have been supported by the culture throughout the industrial age.

INDUSTRIAL AGE FATHERING

With the advent of the Industrial Revolution, men's roles in society and in the family changed radically. Prior to that, an agricultural economy kept men closer to home, where farmers and craftsmen worked. There they could have their sons close by as they worked, having frequent daily contact with them, easily available to teach them about being men. Industrialization changed all that, taking men away from home and into the remote workplace.

This change carried tremendous implications for a man's relationship with his entire family, and in particular his sons. As men went away from home in order to earn a living, mother became the primary agent in raising, teaching, and socializing the male child. This meant that most of us were raised by a woman without intimate, daily contact with a man.

Another sad consequence of the industrialization of life is that men became less and less familiar with the earth and with nature. This in itself is a great wound for men. For your father, the loss of his innate affinity with trees, lakes, and rocks also signaled his removal him from his family. The call was for the conquest of nature to feed our insatiable demand for the questionable fruits of the industrial age. A man had to put aside his connectedness to nature and closeness with his family in order to accommodate the necessity of making a living and thus providing for his family. Not only did the industrial era remove your father from home and from nature, but it offered him little to pass on to you about respect for the larger cycles of the earth and the values that reflected this ancient way of honoring the earth.

A glimpse of the values that our fathers were raised with is provided by Sam Keen in "Why We Fight," an interview in *New Age Journal* (March/April 1991), in which he says:

> [W]e believe that the only things of value are things that we create, make, fabricate. Nature is viewed as raw material that in and of itself is valueless. So we take it

and mold it into products. Traditional cultures, on the other hand, believe that nature is the source of all value. Therefore, we should contemplate it, wonder, respect, and wait upon it. The values of a traditional culture would lead us to say, "Don't do something. Wait. Allow something to grow. Be patient. Let's see what happens." In our culture we consider this a very unmanly thing to do. We want to get on with it and get the job done.

The effects of these distorted values are evident everywhere today, but one of the most devastating of these effects is the way the modern era has taken the father out of the home. A father's presence for more than a brief time in the evenings or on weekends is critical to a boy's development. Yet because the requirements of the industrial age took father away for so much of the time, few of us have had the experience of father being with us much when we were growing up. When father isn't available it becomes difficult for a boy really to know what a man is like. Instead the boy must make assumptions based on the little contact he has had with father, and model himself as a man based on his mother's teachings and on men as portrayed by the media. He learns how to portray himself to others, and image becomes more important than substance.

In "A Gathering of Men," a PBS program in which Bill Moyers interviewed Robert Bly, Bly commented:

When we stand physically close to our father, some- thing—something moves over that can't be described in material terms, that gives the son a certain confi- dence, an awareness, a knowledge of what it is to be male, what a man is. And in the ancient times you were always with your father; he taught you how to do things, he taught you how to farm, he taught you what- ever it is that he did. You learned from him. But you had this sense of being—of receiving a food from him. . . . Now, when the father went out of the house

in the Industrial Revolution, that food ended, and I
think the average American father now spends ten
minutes a day with a son . . . and half of that time is
spent in, "Clean up your room!" . . . So the Industrial
Revolution did not harm the mother-and-daughter relationship as much as it did the father-and-son, because
the mother and daughter still stand close to each other
and have stood close to each other.

A boy has a more difficult time establishing his identity as
a man than a girl does establishing her identity as a woman.
Whereas a little girl's identity as a woman will come from the
mother who gave birth to her, from whose body she came and
who has a similar body, a little boy must learn about his identity
from a man. He has a couple of extra crucial steps to take in
the development of his identity. He must first push away from
mother and then be in consistent contact with a man in order
to learn what it's like to have a man's body, a man's feelings,
a man's spirituality.

When father is remote or isn't in the picture at all, it becomes especially difficult for a boy to make the transition away
from mother and into manhood. Arthur describes how he faced
this difficulty from an early age: "My mom and dad were divorced when I was twelve. Not that it mattered much. He
wasn't around anyway when they did live together. When he
was there all I remember is that he wouldn't do much or say
much. He would mainly sit and read for hours."

As an only child, Arthur recalls having a suffocatingly close
relationship with his mother, one in which he was covertly
expected to meet many of her needs for companionship and
caring. She dominated much of his early life. "I didn't see much
of my father after the divorce. He died when I was seventeen,
and I remember at his funeral just not feeling much of anything
for him. I think by then I had learned to gunnysack my feelings
pretty well."

Arthur has been married for ten years. While he and his
wife, Julie, are the best of friends and get along well most of

the time, their sex life has been nonexistent for the past three years. Arthur has been impotent, and Julie has lost interest. He has repeatedly expressed feeling like a little boy with his wife. He often feels powerless with Julie, which serves as a guise for his unresolved and unexpressed anger toward her and his dom-ineering mother. He is also carrying a tremendous amount of rage beneath his outward appearance of having it all together, much of which is directed at his absentee father. Arthur com-pensates for his sense of powerlessness by working long hours in his job as an executive at an aerodynamics corporation. At his job he feels his power and fulfills many of his needs. The point, however, is not to blame his mother or father for these present problems, but to recognize how much the lack of a strong male in his life to give him the "food" of fathering has influenced his present way of acting out a caricature of what he supposes a man is meant to be.

In thinking about the experience of driving the bulldozer with my father that I described earlier, I feel a mixture of sad-ness and longing. I sometimes wonder what it would have been like if my father had been more affectionate, more available—more "there," both physically and emotionally. I suspect that had he been so, his distance and his drinking would still have been wounding but less damaging than they were. I would have loved to have him hold me, to reassure me with direct eye contact, tough yet compassionate discipline, and clear atten-tion. I wonder what would have happened if he had really known how much I needed him. I wonder what it would have been like as a little boy to consistently *know* I was deeply loved by my father.

I will never know this experience of remembering complete confidence in my father's love for me as a little boy. Yet the more I understand myself as a man and a father, the more I understand my father and *his* father, the more I can see how impossible this fantasy really was. Our fathers and all of us grew up at a time that encouraged men to be remote and inaccessi-ble.

HEALING THE FATHER WOUND

Healing the effects of the distance and remoteness you felt from father will take time. The first step in the healing process is to acknowledge the truth. If your father was—or is—unknown to you, and if he doesn't really know you, then you have a father wound. His remoteness kept him from you. Don't fool yourself by coming up with all sorts of reasons and rationalizations as to why it's okay for you not to *feel* anything about this. Yes, he was probably doing the best he knew how. Yes, he had it worse off than you. Yes, your mother had something to do with it, too. Any or all of these statements may be true, but hanging on to any of them as reasons not to feel the profound loss you experienced will leave you with an unhealed wound. That unhealed wound will, in turn, keep you from yourself, keep you from feeling your emotions fully, keep you from tapping into the deep masculine side of yourself fully, keep you in the shadow of your mother and in the chains of your remote father.

By healing your father wound, by grieving the losses you have felt with father, you begin to break the pattern that started generations ago. You begin to see that your father was wounded as well, and that much of his remoteness and/or his violence was his method of coping with his wounds. Perhaps you will see behind his mask to discover the hurt little boy that he once was, or perhaps he has buried his wounds so deeply that you will never find them. Maybe he will let you in, maybe he won't. Perhaps because of his death it is too late to talk directly with your father. Regardless, you can do the necessary work of healing the wound with or without his participation.

As you do, you can expect to see changes in many areas of your life—your work, your relationships with women, and your friendships with men. You can learn to trust other men, to relax your guard, and to feel things you haven't let yourself feel for years. As I have continued to do this healing work, I have found that my friendships with men have deepened. I now recognize there are times when I truly need the companionship of men. It's difficult to develop truly close and nurturing male friendships without healing the father-son wound. I also note that my relationship with my dad has changed dramatically as a result of this healing work. I love him as I have never loved him before, and I feel blessed that he lived long enough for us to undergo this healing. As to work, I am much more focused and directed, surer that it is my own choice to do what I am doing. As to relationships with women, my work in healing the father wound has helped me be more of who I am in the presence of a woman.

The scariest thing for most of us in confronting this father wound in ourselves is that there's a little boy inside who's deathly afraid that if he were to do so, the last shred of connection to an already distant father will be severed. It's scary to confront this potential severing when our connection is so tentative in the first place. If we express some of our rage and our pain, he may reject us altogether, which would really leave us fatherless. Even if father was violent and mean, it may be difficult to confront our own rage and pain stemming from his brutality, because we have a deep-seated fear of ultimately cutting that tentative link with him.

Grieving As A Path To Healing

One of the steps to becoming a fully mature male is to let go of the father that you have held on to in your mind, whether you think of him as a son-of-a-bitch or a saint, or whether his image is hazy or sharp. Once we have become adults, we carry our fathers inside us as an *introjection*, which is a conglomerate of images and memories of how our fathers were when we were boys. We continue to relate to our fathers as if they still are this internalized image, whether or not they are alive, continuing to form our sense of being a man in reaction to this mental picture.

If your father was a tyrant when you were little, this is still the way you see him in your mind, whether or not you're conscious of it. If you were afraid of him as a little boy, then you can still feel the fear alive inside you today, whether or not your father is living. You may have unintentionally modeled yourself after him in some ways as well, perhaps being tyrannical with your wife or children or with your employees. If he is alive, you likely find yourself still fearful of challenging him or telling him your real feelings, afraid of his disapproval and his temper.

I remember my father as being quite passive except when he was drinking, at which point he could be loud and obnoxious. As a boy, I kept my distance from him. As an adult, I still harbored these two very contrasting images of him. For a good deal of my adult life, I identified with the passivity and noninvolvement much more than I care to admit. I was also very intimidated whenever I was around him, afraid to approach him because I wasn't sure if he'd be there. When he drank, I was angry but never told him about it, because I thought he would really get mad and leave, which I had seen him do when I was little. Then there would be no hope of ever having a relationship as an adult.

Much of the work of healing you need to do has two major parts: first, letting yourself feel the emotions that you suppressed as a child—rage, hurt, anger, sadness, happiness, ecstasy—that is, the full range of emotions that a child would naturally feel; and second, deeply feeling the grief now as a man over what you have lost along the way—your childhood, a close relationship with your father, all the opportunities with him that you missed. If you're like most men, you haven't been used to feeling your emotions deeply, so look for any sign of feeling and its release. The first sign of any feeling will probably be anger, and if you let yourself feel a little more deeply, you will readily find your hurt and pain. In the chapter on emotions there are more specific ideas and exercises to help you open up your emotional channels.

Grieving is the process we go through whenever there is a loss. Once you move through the denial that you have any feelings at all about the loss(es), then you can feel the pain caused by the loss. Anger typically leads the way into the sadness and pain of the loss. Sometimes if you get bogged down in blaming your father, this will keep you angry and prevent you from moving on to the feelings that lie just underneath the anger: the hurt and the sadness. Most of us are conditioned to think it's okay to feel and express anger, but not hurt or sadness.

For the following exercises, I suggest you use a journal not only to perform the exercises but to record any thoughts or feelings that occur to you each day about your father wound or its healing process. It will require a warrior's courage to take this internal journey. Go as deep and as far as you can. If you are in a men's group, share your process with the other members of the group. If not, tell one of your closer friends what you are involved in. This in itself may be tough to do, but be tough and do it. Let someone in. Go for it. You have nothing to lose but your fear of feeling, and much to gain in the way of your freedom to be yourself, unbounded by the chains created in childhood by your relationship with your father.

GRIEVING YOUR FATHER LOSS

In order for a new relationship to develop with your father, you must let him go. No, not so much your actual father if he is still alive, but let go of the old image that is no longer functional. Ultimately, this will be necessary for your healing of the wound. You can learn to accept him for who he really is, not to deny and rationalize his behavior and thus deny yourself your feelings about it, but to say good-bye to the father from your past. This way you can begin to relate to your father, whether he is dead or alive, simply as the man he is or was, man to man, rather than as inner boy to an all-powerful father of the past.

The first step in letting go will be to become more aware of some of the emotions you are presently holding on to about your father, many of which are feelings left over from childhood. The following exercise is designed to help you get in touch with some of these feelings.

Exercise 1: Finding Your Feelings About Father

To help you discover more about your feelings about your dad, below you will find some incomplete sentences. In your journal, write these out one at a time and then add anything that comes to mind that will complete the statement. You may have more than one way to complete a statement. If that's the case, write down each response. As you do so, pay close attention to any emotions that are brought up—anger, fear, sadness, happiness. When you have completed all of these, read them out loud with a man friend or to your men's group.

   1. My father was . . .
   2. My earliest memory of him is . . .
   3. I felt most angry with him when . . .
   4. When I needed him most . . .
   5. He really hurt me when . . .
   6. The main regret I have about our relationship is . . .
   7. I felt scared the most when he . . .
   8. With my mother, my father was . . .
   9. When I was a little boy, my father . . .
   10. The way I am like my father is . . .
   11. What I admired most about him was . . .
   12. The biggest lesson I learned from him was . . .
   13. If I could have changed him, he would have been . . .
   14. My father's biggest frustration was . . .
   15. The experience I missed not having with him was . . .

Perry did this exercise, then read his responses to his friend Adrien. He reports, "When I was writing the sentences out and finishing them, mostly what I felt was anger. I read them to Adrien, and when I did I realized that I had been stuck on my anger with my dad since I was about fourteen years old. What I started feeling when I read them to him was a lot of sadness that I didn't realize was there. I really missed not having a dad who was there for me." In Perry's description it's apparent that he is beginning to grieve more fully the loss of the father he never had.

Exercise 2: Saying Good-bye to Dad

Now that you have some further awareness of your feelings about your father, you can go on to an even more challenging exercise. Before you can get to know the real man behind the mask of your father, it will help to actively release the old image the boy or adolescent inside you carries. To do so use the following visualization. Read it through once. Then, either have someone you trust read it to you, or record it on a cassette and play it while you do the exercise. If you record it, leave pauses for your responses between each sentence. You might even want to record the exercise if someone else is reading it to you. Then, find a comfortable chair to sit on. You'll need to sit up rather than lie down so you have less of a chance of going to sleep. Close your eyes and focus on your breathing. Then proceed:

[Read slowly] Notice your breathing. Feel the sensation of your chest as it rises and falls in rhythm to your exhaling and inhaling. Be aware of any other sensations in your body. Notice the areas that are tight and the areas that are relaxed. As you focus on your breathing, be aware that you are slowly walking down a flight of stairs. With each step you take downward, you feel more relaxed, yet at the same time anticipating that something very important is about to happen.

As you descend the staircase and come close to the bottom, you look up and there is a door. When you come to the bottom of the stairs, you steadily and slowly walk across the floor to the door. Reach out and pull the handle. As the door opens, you see that it is a comfortable room with two chairs in it, plus some other furnishings. The room feels warm and inviting.

There is a figure in one of the chairs. At first you see him only from the back. Then you realize that seated in one of the chairs is your father. Notice how your body feels as you realize this. Move toward the other chair and seat yourself opposite him. You can see clearly that this is your father just as he looked when you were a young boy or a teenager. He is looking directly at you. Notice his eyes, the color of his hair, the features of his face. Observe his clothing. What is he wearing? What about his shoes? Notice the way he is sitting. Be aware of what you are feeling as you look at him. Perhaps it's hard to look him directly in the eyes. Or perhaps he has a hard time looking directly into your eyes.

You find yourself relaxing more deeply even as you feel your feelings more intensely. You realize that it's time to say good-bye to your father, this man that you grew up with, that this will be the last time you see him. You look directly at him and say, "I've come to tell you good-bye, Dad. I've got to go away from you and be my own man. I'll never see you again." *[Pause]*

Hear yourself saying anything else you need to say to him. Let him know your anger. Your hurt. Your regrets. Your thanks. Your love. Whatever you need to say, now's the time to say it, because you won't ever see him again after this. Don't hold back. Tell him the truth about your feelings. He can't hurt you now. All the things that you wanted to say. *[Pause]*

And now, listen to what he says to you—if anything. *[Pause]* When that's complete, look deeply into your father's eyes. As you do, notice what you are feeling. Notice his reaction.

After a bit, stand up and move toward the door. Open the door, pause, turn around and look one more time at your father. Notice the look on his face. Whatever else you need to say, say it now. One final time you look at him and say "Good-bye, Dad." Then, turn and close the door behind you. Be aware of what you are feeling as you walk away from the door to the stairs.

Reflecting on your feelings you climb back up the stairs. Now you notice your awareness returning to the room you are in. Be aware of your body sitting on the surface it's on. Notice your breathing. Take a nice, slow, deep breath, exhaling completely. Whenever you are ready, taking as much time as you need, open your eyes and look around the room you are in. Slowly at first, move your body so you can feel it again and orient yourself. Then quietly pick up your journal and write about what you have just experienced.

Write in your journal about your experience in this closed-eye exercise. How did you feel? Were you able to say good-bye to your dad? Was it easy or difficult? What else did you have to say? Does this change how you feel about your father?

Larry wrote about his experience: "He was the dad I had when I was about sixteen. He stopped the hitting about that time because I was getting too big. When I sat down to look at him, he looked old and brittle. His eyes were looking right at me, but he looked kind of scared. That's the first time I'd ever thought of my father as being afraid. When I said good-bye to him, I felt real uncomfortable, like I wanted to cry but couldn't. As mean as that bastard was to me, I still feel like I love him. I found myself calling him Daddy, which was odd. I told him that I loved him, which I never did when he was alive. The tears are coming as I write this. He was such a grumpy old man. Now I can see how afraid he was behind all this grumpiness and gruffness. It was hard to go through the door and leave him there all alone. That's what he's been his whole life—all alone. I really broke down after that, but it was something I knew I had to do."

Ned went through the exercise and described what happened for him: "I don't recall my father being around much when I was little. I know he was in the service when I was really young, and even after that he just didn't seem to be around much. Anyway, I had a hard time picturing him sitting in front of me. That in itself made me feel really sad. When I started to see his face and body, I got really pissed off because now that I had him there I didn't want to say good-bye. When I did say good-bye to him it really hurt. After the exercise I realized that I have been wishing for the father I never had and never will have, and that I really do need to stop wishing for that. He wasn't there when I was younger and that's really sad."

LETTER TO FATHER

I am a true believer in writing letters to do emotional healing work. One of the more powerful experiences you can have is to write a letter or letters to your dad, whether he is alive or dead. The value of the letter is in the writing, not in the response he will make to it. If he has died, then obviously you will not get a response. If he is alive, it really isn't necessary to give him the letters you write. They are primarily for you, to identify and clear whatever feelings you need to clear. If you do decide to give any letters to your father, be prepared. Do not expect him to be different than he's been most of his life. Do not expect him to be enthusiastic or happy when you tell him the truth through your writing. Do expect yourself to feel uncomfortable. The main principle is not to run from him if you decide to give him one of your letters. Go on to the exercise following this one for some tips.

Exercise 3: Letter to Father

There are two types of letters you can write. The first is a good-bye letter. In my workshops, usually after we've done the visualization of "Saying Good-bye to Dad," the first thing I'll have participants do is write a good-bye letter. You can do this in your journal or on a separate piece of paper. The second type of letter is a feelings letter. In this one you write to your father and let him know unabashedly what you are feeling. You may in fact write several of each over time as you become more aware of the feelings that you have kept hidden for and about your father.

Below is an example of a letter written by Ernie, who opted to write a feelings letter.

Dear Dad,

For most of my life I have looked up to you, admired you, and wanted to be like you. I know you worked hard to support your family, and you didn't take much for yourself. But now I can see how much I really missed you growing up. You weren't there for

me a lot of the time. You were either away at work, or
you were doing something around the house, or fixing
the car. And the times you were with us at home you
were usually quiet, burying your face in a newspaper
or a book. I never realized you were so distant, so
emotionally unavailable. I just thought that's the way
men are.

I see how much I am like you. I was holding your
grandson Todd the other day, and for some reason I
got really teary eyed. He looked at me like I was a
Martian. He's seen me angry, but it was the first time
in his eight years he'd ever seen me crying. Not that
I haven't cried, it's just that I had never let him see
me crying before.

The other day at the park I watched a father and
son playing catch with each other. I felt really sad
because I realized that you and I had never done this.
Never. Mom always came to my baseball games, but I
only remember you coming once. I feel angry about
that. Maybe we can still play a game of catch before
you get too old, Pops.

Love,
Ernie

In one of my workshops, a thirty-eight-year-old man named
Dale did the closed-eye exercise and wrote the following good-
bye letter to his father, who had died ten years before:

Dear Dad,

I have to say good-bye Dad. It seems strange to do
so since you died so long ago. But I never got to say
good-bye to you then. Why did you have to die? I was
just getting to know you, and you went and died. It
doesn't make sense but I'm really mad at you for doing so. I hated going to your funeral. Something you'll
never know is how I cried afterward, all by myself. I

couldn't let anybody else see me cry, because I had to
be strong—just like you.

When I did the exercise I could see you as clear
as day sitting in that rocking chair across from me.
You were looking right at me, and I kept wanting to
look away. Then it was time for me to get up and leave
and to say good-bye to you. I didn't like having to do
it. I feel ripped off by your dying and going away. I
don't think you ever really knew me—your very own
son. There were times I hated you and times I admired
you, and sometimes I even loved you.

Now it's time to say good-bye to you and let you
go. It's scary to do this, but I must do it. My heart
hurts. I'm sitting here in this workshop as I write
this, crying up a storm. I hate to leave you, but I have
to. Thanks for being my dad. You weren't perfect, but
you gave me a good start, and I'll always remember
you.

Love,
Dale

Another example of a letter is one that I did recently. I
have done a fair amount of work on my own father wound, yet
every so often I find some feelings that are up for review and
release. Just recently I did some emotional work that had to do
with releasing my pattern of passivity and passive-aggressiveness
with woman. As I worked with a counselor, it became apparent
that much of this was rooted in the modeling I did with my
father, specifically the one I had internalized. After doing some
anger work where I pounded some pillows, growled, and deeply
felt my anger and hurt at my father's emotional distance, I
wrote the following letter later that day:

Dear Dad,

I hated you when you drank. When you did I was
really scared of you. I would always run off to my
bedroom because I didn't know what else to do. You

taught me to be afraid of my own power because when I saw it in you it would always hurt others and be painful. I made a rule that I would never get angry because then I would be like you when you were angry—hurtful and out of control.

And when you weren't drinking you just weren't there. A lot of times you would just fall asleep in your stupid chair. I wish you had held me, talked with me, whispered to me, read me bedtime stories. Nighttimes were always the scariest, especially when you and Mom had one of your fights.

I never knew you. How do I know how to be a man? There's only two pictures I have of you. One is of you being quiet and shy, not saying much, even at home. The other is where you were angry and loud. That's how I saw you being with Mom. You were either fighting with her or else passive and submissive. I hated it when I would ask you something and you wouldn't make a decision yourself, but instead you would say, "Go ask the boss." Where were your balls? I also don't remember your touching Mom at all. I can't think of any times when you two hugged, held hands, or kissed, other than in a perfunctory way. It was either fighting or distance. That was my picture of how to be with a woman.

Dad, I really do love you, and I'm glad you're still alive. I need to know you more. I need to feel with you. I need to know your pain, your anger, and your love.

Steven

There was a lot of emotion when I wrote this letter, and a sort of rawness that is typical of how you can write your letter to your father. Choose which type of letter you want to write, then write it. Don't think about it a lot or try to compose it so it reads well. Just write it. When you are done, put it aside for a few days. Writing the letter will undoubtedly bring up some things that you may want to actually say to your father now if he is living. After a few days rewrite it. If you choose, you can send this second letter to your father or read it to him next time you are with him.

If you do send it or read it, be prepared. Your father may listen, or he may totally deny what you have written. It's best to be realistic about the outcome. The purpose of writing this letter is primarily for you—to allow you to grieve the loss of the father you didn't have, not to get him to change to be a more ideal father. If you do share it with him, remind yourself that you are dealing with the man he is today, not the father of the past. Also remind yourself that you are an adult son, and no longer this man's child.

The next exercise is to help you heal the father wound—having a talk with your father.

TALKING WITH YOUR FATHER

If your father is alive, you have the opportunity to open up the relationship by approaching him and talking straightforwardly with him. If your father has died, you can adapt this exercise by either talking with a friend and having him role play your father, or by taking an empty chair and pretending your father is sitting in it. While you may feel uncomfortable doing this with your friend or with a chair, get through your discomfort and do it anyway. It will be a learning experience. If your father is alive, it may help to rehearse what you want to say by going through it with a friend or an empty chair.

Exercise 4: Role Playing: Talking with Father

Imagine your father is sitting across from you in a chair. Make direct eye contact. Speak slowly and clearly. What are you feeling? What do you want him to know about you? Are there any situations from childhood that you need to address?

If this were actually your father, what would you want to

know about him? About his past? How did he meet your mother? What was one of his greatest adventures? What was his relationship with his father like?

Tell him about your anger, hurt, sorrow, joy. Let him get to know you, especially your insides. What are your hopes and dreams? How do you feel right now being with him?

Lonnie recruited his friend Wesley to sit in as his father when he tried this exercise. Lonnie described his rehearsal: "Wes was perfect as my father. My dad was really strict and critical. He expected nothing less than A's on my report cards. I suppose he was doing it to try and make me succeed, but it was a real drag most of the time. Lots of times he would make me stay at home when all of my friends were going out.

"When we rehearsed, I told my dad—Wes—about this, and Wes reacted just like my dad would have. He told me that I was wrong for feeling that way, that he did it for my own good. But the difference this time was that I was able to get angry. I even surprised myself, and Wes too. I really told him off, and it felt good to stand up to my dad for a change. I went on to tell him that I felt really stifled by him. I also got a glimpse of why he was that way. I know his father was the same way with him, even worse than he was with me. Once I saw this I could feel more appreciative for what he did. Dad gave it his best shot, and I know he loved me in the only way he knew how."

Corby tried this with an empty chair. "I felt kind of silly at first, until I closed my eyes. I got a very strong picture of him sitting across from me. I opened my eyes, and it was like he was actually there. The first thing I felt was sad. He always looked so worn out. I told him so, and went on to tell him how his work always got in the way between him and me. He had his own business, and as far back as I can remember, he was always working, if not at the shop, then at home. I told him how I'd always felt shut out, and that I didn't like his not including me in some way when I was younger, even if it was to go to the shop with him and do some little jobs here and there. I went on to tell him how sad it was to see him put his work first, even before his family. It seemed he was even nicer and friendlier to the people at the shop than he was to his own family. I feel really bad that he wasn't more available."

From here you may want to move on to the next step. If and when you are ready, set up a time when you can actually talk with your dad. If you expect it to be particularly difficult, you can recruit a friend as support to talk with before and afterward. Then say what you need to say—and be willing to truly listen to what your dad is saying. There's no need to be right about what you are saying, but be willing to say it with some forcefulness and intensity. Remember, this could be one of the scariest things you've ever done, because you are meeting him as a man rather than a regressed little boy. Don't hide. Go for it.

I recall a significant communication with my dad, one that opened the door for a new way of relating to him. This was a few years ago, when I confronted my father about his drinking. I had heard from my brother that Dad was on one of his drinking streaks again. He would increase his drinking around holidays and summertime, and have a bout of drinking steadily for several weeks at a time. I had also heard that he had taken my two children, Nicole and Catherine, in his truck with him when he had been drinking. I was furious when I heard the news. I knew I had to confront him and set some limits. Although my dad and I had discussed his drinking before, it was usually in a very offhanded way and we would move to another subject rather quickly. I was determined that this wouldn't happen this time.

I went to my parents' house, walked in, and sat down. There was a brief exchange of some usual opening conversations: How were the children, my mother's concerns about social matters in the trailer park where they lived, some talk about how the

Rams were going to do that Sunday. Then I got down to business.

"Dad, I want to talk with you about your drinking." I must have said it with considerable resolve, because my dad looked squarely at me, and my mom offered to leave and go in the other room.

"No, Mom," I continued, "I want you here to listen to what I have to say. Dad, I'm really angry. I heard that you were driving with Nicole and Catherine in the truck after you had been drinking. I don't want you to ever do that again!"

He neither denied it nor agreed to it. He kept looking at me as I continued. "In fact, your drinking has been a problem for me for some time, and I need to do something about it."

He countered with, "Well, don't you have a beer now and again?"

"Yes I do, once in a while, but that's not the point. The point is that your drinking has gotten to be a problem. I realize that I can't make you stop, and I don't care to. Your union has programs to help you, or you can go to AA, if you're ready to do something about it. But I can't make you. I'm just really tired of being around you when you're drinking. You change. You get louder. You're hard to be around."

My mother offered, "Maybe that's why you were so shy when you were little?" She was intuitively on the mark with that comment.

"I went on, "Yeah, I'm sure that was a lot of it. I was afraid whenever you drank, Dad. I never really knew you. I just remember your drinking a lot. And I hated the fights you two got into."

My dad looked away for a few moments, and I think I caught his eyes tearing up. "I don't know what to say. I usually have a couple of beers when I get home."

"It's not just the one or two beers, Dad." I was determined not to buy into his denial. "It's the pattern that goes on. You go along fine for a while, and then you start drinking, and do it regularly. That's when I don't like being around you. In fact, I'm not willing to be around you any more when you've been drinking. From here on, before I come over, I'm going to call. If you've been drinking, let me know—I can usually tell anyway. If you have, then I won't come by. If you haven't, great. Then I will come by. And I refuse to bring the girls anywhere near you if you have."

We had some further discussion, a little less tense, about alternatives he had for treatment and recovery. He never really followed through, nor did my mother. But something shifted for me in talking with my father in this way, from confronting him from a position of being clear on my boundaries and what I wanted. It was one of the first times I felt like I faced him man to man.

Talking with your father, whether it's actually him or the image of him, can help you heal the father-son wound. It can open the door for the necessary grieving to release your father from being a parent to you as a child, and instead help you see him as a man who is carrying his own wounds.

BOTH A SON AND A FATHER

In a recent conversation with my father, I was telling him about my concerns with my younger daughter, Catherine, now eight years of age.

ME: I see how Catherine has learned to hide her feelings. She's carrying a lot of hurt, but she doesn't show it. To most people she comes across as just being shy, but sometimes she has this wall around her that's hard to get through.

DAD: You were a lot like that. You'd never let me get close to you. Every time I'd go to pick you up, you would cry or run away.

ME: Well, Catherine hasn't been quite that extreme. I'm sure I was pretty difficult to get through to. Still, I know I'm going to have to go get her at times and insist that she come out from behind her wall.

DAD: Well, maybe, but you were really hard to get to.

ME: Yes, but I wish you had come and gotten me. It pisses me off that you didn't. Even if I was hard to get to, I wish you had sometimes just scooped me up and held me, even if I was kicking and screaming. I don't like that you held back so much. It would probably have helped.

I didn't feel the need to blame my dad or make him wrong, but I did feel my anger over this exchange. I didn't know what his response would be, so I was pleasantly surprised when he simply said, "You're probably right." It felt good that he acknowledged my feelings, and I learned some things about myself both as a son and as a father.

This conversation is rich with evidence of the father wound. It was also an important step for me in healing that wound. Since I am both a son and a father I can feel my own woundedness with my father as well as appreciate how my two daughters have in their own way been hurt. While I've not been sexually or physically abusive, their woundedness has come from my habit of being emotionally unavailable in their earlier years. I see now that it is impossible for children not to suffer some sort of woundedness from their fathers.

Adam, a close friend of mind, has acknowledged that he has wounded his thirteen-year-old son, Paul. By his own admission, Adam has been distant and unavailable as a father until recently, and sees in Paul the same emotional distance that he once had. In a group that I shared with Adam, Paul, and some other fathers and sons, Adam looked directly at Paul and confessed to him, haltingly, with tears in his eyes and a sob in his throat, "I never wanted to hurt you. I feel so bad about the times I've yelled at you and hit you. Just the other day I found a picture of you when you were only three days old. I remember looking at you when you were just a baby and promising myself that I'd never hurt you. And I have. And I'm sorry, son." At this point Adam broke down, overcome by his grief at how he had failed in his promise.

Paul listened carefully, displaying little outward response. After some prodding, Paul admitted that he didn't trust his dad because he had broken promises before. He also admitted that it was only the second time he had ever seen his dad cry, so it was new to him. Some time later, Paul experienced his own grief and, while being held by another man in the group, sobbed the deep sorrow of a young man who was only now grieving his own father wound.

Michael Meade, a reknowned storyteller who has been very active in leading men's gatherings, in an interview for a periodical called *The Sun* entitled "On Being A Man," recounted:

> When I first became a father, I said, "I'm not going to do what my father did." That's one of the first fantasies of a father. "I'm going to do this right." Another father fantasy, "I'm not going to make all the mistakes. And I'm not going to hurt my children." Well, it doesn't turn out that way at all. The more I dwelt on that, the more I realized that it's inevitable. Wounds are part of what parents give to their children.
>
> Fatherhood is generous, but this generosity is indiscreet. Fathers give of themselves, and they give their wounds, too. So every son is wounded by the father. Every daughter is wounded by the father. Part of the business of living is healing those wounds. By "healing" I don't mean getting rid of them. Sometimes a wound needs to be opened and cleansed, and scar tissue needs to develop.

And this is exactly what it will take for you to heal your father wound. To do so requires you to summon up your warrior's courage and focus inward for this journey, venturing into the dark spaces inside you that you had not previously explored—especially the dark space of your relationship with your father. Although the ideas outlined above are certainly not exhaustive in terms of healing the father wound, they are a beginning.

Next we will look even more closely at how we as men have learned to shut down our emotions, then explore specific ways to open them up again.

3

A Man and His Feelings: Shut 'em Down and Put 'em Away

I've spent many years of my life shut down emotionally, afraid and unwilling to be close to others. I figured that intimacy between a man and a woman is what happened in the bedroom. And forget being intimate with another man—that was out of the question. I've been through two marriages and several relationships and have found myself trapped in each one by my fear of getting too close and by my inability to let go of my rigid controls over my emotions. I had feelings—very deep feelings—but I didn't have a clue about what to do with them. They scared the hell out of me. Sometimes they hurt me; sometimes, when I acted them out, they hurt others. It seemed a lot safer not to feel anything, or at least not to let anyone know what I was feeling.

I remember sadly how my first wife and I rarely talked about our feelings. Beth and I had been married for a few months, and up to that time had expressed our love and caring physically, through sex. Although I loved her—at least as much as I was capable of loving someone at that time—I had dared not venture from behind my emotional walls to tell her so. It was too risky; she might have hurt me if I were to be so boldly vulnerable. When I did express any feelings, I felt I quickly had to minimize them so I would stay safe.

In bed one day as we were resting in each other's arms after making love, I felt a tremendous surge of affection and caring for her, but I didn't know what to do with it. I struggled inside for several minutes, making small talk, keenly aware of both my tender feelings toward her and my unease at feeling them. After experiencing much trepidation, I finally looked directly at her, and mustering all my courage, blurted out, "I love you." Without thinking much about it, I just as quickly added, "But I'll get over it," thereby effectively canceling any warmth or affection in the first part of the statement, and keeping me safe from any rejection. I laughed right after I said it, and so did she, nervously deflecting the discomfort at my having been so bold and so cowardly in the same breath. What was even more tragic is that this became a running joke between us. Any time after that, whenever one of us would say to the other, "I love you," the standard comeback was, "You'll get over it." It saddens me to realize just how shut down I have been in my life, how afraid I have been of the most natural thing in the world—feelings.

In fact, for the longest time, the only feelings that I found at all acceptable were anger and lust. When I felt these and expressed them, I didn't have to risk being vulnerable, being exposed. I could express my anger by hitting walls or by acting it out in some passive-aggressive way such as pretending I wasn't angry when I really was, then getting even by not talking with my spouse for several days. All the time I would lie through gritted teeth and deny that I was angry, outwardly expressing puzzlement as to why she was having such a problem.

Lust became a refuge wherein I could actually feel something intensely. When I was having sex I could meet my needs for touch, for release, and—even if it was only briefly—my need to feel loved and cared for. I could let my guard down to some degree and express myself, at least through my body. The more I closed down my feelings in the rest of my life, the more important sex became as a means to feel.

FROZEN FEELINGS

I know that I am like most other men in the way I have dealt
with emotions, if not in the specifics, then certainly in the
general way of not knowing what to do with these things called
feelings. One popular option for us is to stop feeling altogether,
to put our feelings away so—it's hoped—we won't have to deal
with them. In fact one of the most pronounced effects of our
wounds is that we learn to numb our emotions, and as a result
most of us have grown up with a huge wad of cotton around
our feelings.

This emotional numbing started very early in childhood,
and continues on into adulthood. We learn distorted rules about
manhood while growing up in our families, particularly about
keeping our feelings under control. These messages continue to
be disseminated through peers, school, work, television, movies,
and advertising to the extent that we cannot help but be influenced, to conclude that this is the way we are supposed to
behave as men. In our culture, men simply are not supposed to
feel. Instead, we are supposed to deny our emotions, remain
numb, and keep a stoic look on our faces at all times. This has
been the traditional ideal of manhood. While it may have
worked for our ancestors, it's evident that it isn't working for
us anymore.

By remaining emotionally numb you may *seem* to avoid
pain, but at the same time you avoid love and joy. When you
deaden yourself to grief, you also deaden yourself to ecstasy.
When we were children we naturally felt a whole range of emotions, but because of cultural strictures on feelings, and specifically on boys' expressing feelings, we had learned to be
nonexpressive and shut down by the time we were seven years
old. Now in adulthood, we take great measures and spend lots
of energy continuing to mask our feelings. Our long-standing
grief and pain beg for acknowledgment and release, but until
we are willing to take the necessary steps to open up—covered
in the next chapter—then we continue to suffer in silence.

The cost of remaining shut down can be tremendous. Only through your feelings can you relate intimately with another person. When you are distant from your feelings, you remain distant from others, even the people you love. The longer the emotional walls stay up, the more you risk ending up isolated and friendless. In addition, when you don't have effective ways to deal with your anger and rage, they can spill out indiscriminately upon those around you, or be hidden away, frozen behind the mask of depression. To remain closed off from your feelings is to objectify and dehumanize yourself, leaving yourself in an all-too-familiar state of detachment and inaccessibility—just like your father.

I'm not sure I can convince you that it's better to open up. It's risky and it hurts, especially at first. All of the pain and suffering you have worked so hard to keep under cover will usually be the first feelings to surface, although with the deep release of these you will also feel relief and perhaps even joy and ecstasy. Opening up your feelings requires consistent work and attention. It is not done in one grand cathartic splash, even though you may have that kind of experience. What does come as you open your feelings is a greater sense of being alive, of being connected with others, particularly those you love. If you have children, it will bring you closer to them and you will, no doubt, appreciate them even more. You will rediscover the passion and life that are at the core of your being, and that were innately yours when you first came into this world. Moreover, if I haven't convinced you yet, your orgasms will be much more intense. But you have to determine for yourself whether or not it's worth it to get committed to opening up.

First let's explore further how we shut our feelings down and how we maintain an emotional numbness.

CHILDHOOD LESSONS

When you are a child you are particularly susceptible to adult authority, and will instinctively do whatever is necessary to survive. If experiencing very natural emotions, such as crying when you are hurt or expressing outrage when a parent does something harmful to you, means that you may be hurt further, then you instinctively cut yourself off from these emotions. These wounds—whether they be from physical battering, words that shame, or a parent who withdraws love in response to your emotional expression—lead you to conclude that it's not okay to feel. Since you were a boy, there was typically even more pressure on you to "take it" and not react, especially by crying. Like many other men, you may have been told "big boys don't cry" on more than one occasion. Once you have learned these lessons as a child they settle into your body; automatically you keep your feelings frozen, on into adulthood. It becomes an ingrained habit.

Phil is forty-nine years old and has been married and divorced twice. He came to counseling mainly because he's considering a third marriage and is committed to making sure that he's ready this time. "My last wife had the same complaint as the first one—that the only feelings I seemed to show were my anger and rage. The last fight we had I got so angry with her I took a glass jar that we had bought in Europe and shattered it on the floor. It was costly, in more ways than one—and to tell you the truth, it felt pretty good at the time. But I felt really bad afterwards. I guess that was the last straw for her. She left that night, and soon after started the divorce proceedings. Don't get me wrong, she was no angel. It's just that I can really see how closed up I've been, how much I used anger to keep her away. I wouldn't—no, *couldn't* let her see what else I was feeling. I didn't know how." Phil had learned to steel himself, not to let his wife in, and even to push her away with his anger. To understand the source of his way of masking his feelings, we have to look back into Phil's childhood.

Phil recalls how his mother would continuously shame and

criticize him: "She wouldn't stop. She would pick, pick, pick. 'Your hair's getting too long'; 'you didn't do the lawn right'; 'what are you doing hanging around with that girl?' I couldn't do anything right in her eyes. I learned to keep my feelings to myself. One time when I was about twelve years old I was roller-skating with some friends of mine. I stayed a little longer than I was supposed to. She came down to the skating rink and yelled my name while I was out on the floor. That embarrassed the hell out of me, but she didn't stop there. While I was changing my skates, with all my friends around, she was raking me over the coals, putting me down. I got really mad at her, but I couldn't say anything because she would just come back at me twice as strong. There was a cute girl there that I had been trying to impress, too—I guess she really was impressed after my mom got done with me! For weeks after that I couldn't face that girl at school, and my friends teased me endlessly."

It was easier for Phil not to say anything than to speak up. He learned to blunt his anger toward is mother along with any other feelings. His suppressed anger came out in his rage with each of his wives; any other emotions felt too dangerous to reveal, so he bottled them up.

Because Phil's father was passive and uninvolved, there was little support for him there. In fact, his father's lack of involvement provided further reinforcement for Phil to emulate this remote behavior when he reached manhood. By his own account, his inaccessibility—reminiscent of his father's—was the chief complaint of both of Phil's previous wives.

Even if our fathers were physically present in the home, most of us witnessed very little emotional expression on their part. Someone once quipped that a man has two feelings: quiet and angry. If your father did express emotion, it was most likely anger. With such an exemplar of so-called manly behavior, it's no wonder that you have found yourself emotionally constricted in adulthood.

Your family provided the original training and role models for how you, as a boy and later as a man, were supposed to deny and detach yourself from your feelings. However, your family was the purveyor of values that came from the larger culture within which you grew up. Our culture has tended to support values that maintain our denying and adapting to our woundedness rather than encouraging our healing. Our culture not only proffered those values when we were boys, but sustained them on into manhood through various rules and rituals.

CULTURAL LESSONS

Most of us harbor a generalized fear of our feelings, the notable exception to this being anger. The training and influences we received as boys stay with us into adulthood until we make an active effort to challenge these conditioned fears and learn to experience a whole range of emotions again. By our healing we are not only overcoming our family rules, we are overcoming certain cultural values with which we have grown up and that simply do not support our healing. There are four main widespread cultural values that support our fears of feeling our emotions more intensely and of more openly expressing these feelings: competitiveness, overvaluation of rationality, fear of vulnerability, and rugged individualism.

Competitiveness

In our culture, competitiveness is prized over cooperation. It permeates the entire society, from the education system to corporate life. To echo the words of Vince Lombardi, the famous coach of the championship Green Bay Packer football teams of the 1960s, "Winning isn't everything; it's the only thing." Men are cast in either/or categories of winners and losers. When this attitude prevails, aggression and domination become the prime traits that are rewarded. Sensitivity and vulnerability are forbidden in this type of system, in large part because to exhibit such traits leaves you open to being trodden upon by your competitors.

That's not to imply that there's anything wrong with competition. Games between men are fun and entertaining and can serve as ritual ways to focus the competitive need. I know very few men who don't enjoy some type of competition. Unfortunately, competition is unduly prized and taken far beyond ritualized fun and entertainment into the realm of the workplace and personal relationships. It's the "killer" attitude behind such competition that hurts and divides, that turns people into winners and losers. When winning and losing is taken seriously, where there are implications that the winner is somehow better and the loser is less of a man, then it further stifles any freedom of expression between participants.

This competitive attitude has predominated for centuries. It has revealed itself in a basic attitude about the earth and nature with which we have grown up. In Western culture particularly, we have viewed the forces of nature and the earth itself from this competitive standpoint, as entities to be wrestled with and dominated, rather than things with which to harmonize and to cooperate. Not only does this attitude serve to repress and control human emotions, but it attempts to repress and control the natural flow of life here on earth.

In most businesses where this competitive spirit prevails, it becomes extremely difficult, if not altogether impossible, for a man to be at all open with his feelings. Frank has worked for a number of years in a management position in a corporation. In a group he described some of the inherent dangers of being expressive of feelings in a business situation where this competitive attitude and all it implies are givens. "When I was first separated [from my wife] I was really torn apart. I have a couple of friends at work whom I've done a lot with. We've worked on projects together. I've played racquetball with them, and gotten together with them for a couple of beers after work. One day while we were having lunch together, I started telling them about being separated and how lonely it was—I think I even started getting tears in my eyes—and they started teasing me about it and laughing. I was really hurt but I didn't dare show it. I started laughing too and just swallowed what I was feeling. I just can't do that sort of thing where I work. If you show any weaknesses, the other guys will walk right on over you."

Overvaluing Rationality

One cultural attitude that has prevailed for the past few centuries—especially in Western civilization—is that rational thinking and behavior are far superior to any other system. It's been generally accepted that reason will conquer all. Emotions have been considered something to be tolerated—something for women and children, but not for men. Logical and analytical thinking, based on rationality, have been prized over intuitive, nonlinear ways of thinking, which are based in the body and directly involve the emotions.

Rationality is considered to be a masculine trait, while emotionalism is felt to be a feminine trait. If you are a man in this culture, then in order to be identified as such you have had to rely heavily on this kind of thinking, thereby squelching your emotional life. For a man to be emotional is this "age of reason" would typically call into question his manhood. This cultural polarization of masculine and feminine characteristics has led to definitions of manhood that exclude any strong showing of feelings and rely on rational thought as the primary mode of operating. According to this system, the more detached from your feelings you are, the more you rely on your rational thinking, the more manly you are.

Rational thought and its offspring, scientific thinking, certainly have had their value. Most of modern technology has sprung from this mode of thinking. Disconnected from intuitive thinking, which has at its foundation our physical sensations and emotional feelings, it becomes dispirited, without real passion or aliveness. Maintaining this approach to life may seem to shield us from pain, but ultimately it doesn't.

Joseph describes how he had to confront this in his own life: "I've always prided myself on my ability to think my way through situations. I figured that most of my problem emotions—depression, guilt, or any kind of unhappiness—were always the result of irrational thinking. I thought I could think my way through any feeling, discover its irrational premise, and from there I would be fine. It wasn't until I nearly lost my son—he was in a serious auto accident—that my feelings all came crashing down around me. I couldn't control them anymore. I felt terrified at the prospect of losing him, and spent a lot of time crying. Fortunately, he was all right, but it was quite an introduction into some feelings that I didn't know I was capable of having."

Fear of Vulnerability

This one is simple. If you don't feel, then you can't be hurt. But if you do, then you risk being hurt. You might be teased and taunted, put down, or perhaps taken advantage of. As boys we learned this very early on. To show any vulnerability means you risk being thought of or even called a "sissy" or a "pussy," and no man wants to risk being labeled and chastised as such. For a man to show his fear or his hurt in front of another man, to truly share it and not just intellectualize it, is risky business. To do so means you are putting what has been traditionally identified as masculine at stake. This is one of the reasons that many men, if they do show any vulnerability, will reveal it to a woman rather than another man.

Yet, to reiterate, as much as there are risks in being vulnerable, there is tremendous cost in the alternative. By avoiding vulnerability, you keep yourself emotionally closed. By not risking, you face the greater risk of keeping yourself isolated and friendless. You may stay safe, but ultimately face the consequences of being disconnected and remote.

A man's grasp on his emotional realm is often so fragile that to be vulnerable is out of the question. Tyler describes his fear of emotions as it relates to vulnerability. "I've always liked talking to women more than men. It seems like I can let down a lot more. I was with a male friend, Ben, the other day, talking about how much I missed my children and that I don't like seeing them every other weekend. Tears started welling up in my eyes. Up to then it seemed like he was listening to me, asking questions. When I started getting close to some hurt, he started talking about some statistics he had read about single parents. He went on and on about this, and stopped making eye contact as he did. It was obvious he was uncomfortable. And of course, me, I didn't push it. I just felt hurt and went right along with the program and got just as superficial as he did. He's still a good friend; it's just that now I'm nervous about opening up with him again."

Rugged Individualism

This cultural standard is a throwback to the pioneering days, when to open frontiers a man had to be detached and hardened and exemplify qualities like courage and strength at the sacrifice of all other feelings. We still see this influence today in our admiration for men who are lone wolves, who stand out and away from the crowd and most awesomely contain and shut off their feelings. The iconization of this type of man has largely occurred through images portrayed in films and on television. I myself must confess some admiration for Clint Eastwood. Many of the characters he has played, such as the "lonesome cowboy" in his earlier westerns or Harry Callahan of the Dirty Harry movies, appeal to that part in me that still identifies with rugged individualism. That's one of the reasons he has been such a popular star and why his movies have generally done so well.

There is, after all, something to be admired about the qualities that make up what we consider the rugged individual. Detachment, courage, strength, individuality, and the pioneering spirit—all are attributes that can be extremely valuable, especially when they serve a purpose that goes beyond self-centered motives. It takes such attributes for a man to stand above the crowd and make a statement. Gandhi, Martin Luther King, George Washington, and Nelson Mandela are some examples of men who embody this kind of rugged individualism that can stimulate and inspire.

When taken to a rigid extreme, however, this value of rugged individualism leads us to be needless, unfeeling, and aloof. Hal has prided himself on his ability: "I've always thought that I didn't need anybody and that feelings were a waste of time. Anybody who disagreed with me was a wimp. Then a couple of years ago I shattered my right leg on my motorcycle and it forced me to lay low for a long time. During that time a couple of things happened. One is that a lot of my friends were really there for me, and it surprised the hell out of me. At first I didn't know how to take it, because I wasn't used to something like that. The second is that it gave me time to really look at my life, and see just how alone and lonely I've been. Sure, I can take care of myself—I know that. Now, the question is, can I let myself be cared for by others?"

Another powerful element that the culture contributes to our messages about manhood are rites of passage that move us out of boyhood and initiate us into manhood.

FROM THE OUTSIDE IN: INITIATION

When girls become women, there is a natural physiological change that takes place from the inside out with the onset of menstruation. This change doesn't have to be forced through ritual or confrontation, nor does a girl have to prove somehow that she's become a woman. For girls, in many primitive societies, ceremony and ritual are used to celebrate and commemorate the spiritual significance of this event, even though a girl's bodily changes themselves clearly mark this passage into womanhood.

Unlike girls, however, boys require intervention from the outside to mark this passage. We need to have something happen that physically helps us move out of the domain of mother's authority and puts us squarely into the world of men. Primitive societies typically had prescribed initiation rites that helped the boy make this transition more quickly. These rites had a spiritual emphasis in that they would teach the boy to have an equal

appreciation for both the spiritual and material world. Through
initiation the boy would come to recognize that there was a
reality much larger than himself; he would be tutored in this
lesson by a spiritual mentor, an older man to guide him through
this passage. He would also learn the ways and values of men
in his culture through stories and fables that clearly conveyed
what it meant to be a man in that particular culture. Out of his
initiation a boy would develop the characteristics of toughness,
courage and fearlessness—all extremely valuable assets.

Although each primitive society had its unique rituals of
initiation, there were common elements. In *What Men Are Like*,
John A. Sanford and George Lough describe the shared features:

> Typically, as the initiation rite begins, the boy is
> taken away from the mother's household to a special
> place set aside only for the men. During the time of his
> initiation, which may last several days, he is systemat-
> ically alienated from his family, and after his initiation
> he is forbidden to return to his mother. The rite itself
> involves enduring physical pain amounting in many
> cases to torture, and also psychological pain engendered
> by the frightening and intimidating nature of the rites.
> *The boy's ability to endure the pain and fear is a hallmark
> of his readiness to enter into the world of men* [emphasis
> added]. His entry into the world of men provides him
> with a new set of relationships to replace the ones he
> has severed. He is also initiated into the "men's mys-
> teries," a body of myth and culture known only to the
> men, and this gives him a new spiritual orientation.

It's sad but true that our culture lacks any such clear initiation rites for males; there remains an apparent need for this
kind of introduction into the world of men. As a result other
types of rituals in our culture fulfill some of the intent of initiation rites, while still falling far short of the kind of spiritual
mentoring and reorienting found in the initiation rites of other

cultures. Rituals such as fraternity hazings, military boot camp, and gang induction trials all have some elements in common with so-called primitive initiation rites.

One of the common elements is the requirement that a boy must prove himself by going through some painful ordeal without showing his fear or his pain. By successfully completing this ordeal, he comes out the other "side" being a man, acknowledged for his male virtues of courage and fearlessness. Thus he learns that to be a man you keep your fear to yourself and do not show your feelings. Unfortunately, since in our culture there is no spiritual mentoring and no one to teach the boy about "men's mysteries," no one to tell him how a man is supposed to feel, he simply shuts off his feelings without having any clue what it means to do so. So, although these initiation rites can teach a boy self-control, courage, and toughness, what receives overemphasis is the suppression of feelings. And even though those rites of passage that do exist in our culture are either extremely diluted or distorted and shortsighted, they still give a boy the very distinct message that being a man means you do *not* show your feelings.

Although I've never been in the military, from men I've talked with about it, boot camp is an example of one such ritual. Juvenile gangs usually have rituals in which the young teenager must pass certain tests of "manhood" in order to become a member of the gang. These trials usually involve an act of bravado in which there is some risk. Whether in the marines or a street gang, a new recruit exhibiting any fear is ridiculed, shamed, and severely chastised by the others.

For some of us, athletics served as the initiation into manhood. One of my rites of passage was through playing football. In spite of my humiliating encounter with baseball when I was younger, I had always thought that I might play football. I discovered in eighth grade that I was fast, so I decided to give it a try once I was old enough.

My first opportunity to try out for football came when I was in tenth grade, when I joined the sophomore team. After going through the necessary physical examination, I reported to the locker room. I watched carefully how the other guys put their football gear on, trying to act as though I knew what I was doing. I didn't know anyone else on the team, since my parents and I had just moved to the city shortly before school began, and my shyness, newness, and nervousness kept me from being too friendly with anyone.

Trying on the uniform for the first time, I got my shoulder pads on backwards. One of the coaches came by and very tactfully suggested that I turn them around. Finally, after a lot of struggle, I cinched the drawstring in my pants, tied my shoes, and left the locker room to go to my first practice. I was the last one out on the field because I had gotten my gear on late, and I walked out to join the other guys in their warm-up calisthenics. As I was stretching I felt totally scared, thrilled, and ecstatic to the bones, all at the same time. But could I show it? No, not at all. There was a very powerful pressure, an unspoken rule felt by us all, that said, "Now you are to keep your feelings to yourself. Do not cry out in pain. Be tough. Be strong. You are training for battle." It was my first experience with this modern version of "warrior training." I instinctively knew something important was happening to me; I suspect that right about then if someone had put hot irons on my forearms I would have tried to grit my teeth, keep my eyes wide open, and stifle *any* sound that even faintly suggested I hurt.

After the calisthenics, we were then instructed to get into groups according to what position we were to be playing. Coach Kennedy then had us pair up. I just happened to pair up with Roy Crabtree, one of the starting tackles, who at six feet, one inch and 175 pounds, was one of the largest, strongest "boys" on the team. Then the coach outlined what we were to do. When he blew the whistle, one of us was to slap our partner on the face with an open hand—this being done, of course, while we were not wearing our helmets.

I'm not sure if I flinched when Coach Kennedy made this unexpected announcement, but I did my best to maintain my cool. Roy and I continued to make eye contact, and he made a slight gesture forward with his head to indicate, "Why don't you go first?" I was relieved to do so, to postpone the inevitable moment when I would be on the receiving end of this assignment.

There was an interminable pause between when the coach assigned this task and when I heard him say, "Ready!" followed by the blast of the whistle. I was standing with my right hand raised, opened up as if to salute Roy. When the whistle shrieked, I cut through the air between Roy's left cheek and my right hand and *whap!* I did it! Roy may have blinked, but if he did I missed it. His left cheek did not even redden. As I realized that I had done it and that he hadn't foamed at the mouth and leapt at me to strangle me, I felt a wave of relief. This lasted for about three seconds, until Coach Kennedy walked up and said, "Nah, Farmer. I said hit him, not caress him."

Then Coach Kennedy said the words that made my heart stop briefly and quickly caused me to reconsider whether my years of waiting to play this game had all been a fierce delusion. He said, "Roy, why don't you show Farmer how you want to be hit?" At this point Roy, without hesitation, raised his open hand and quickly and solidly belted my right cheek. I was jolted by the suddenness of it, and by just how hard Roy had slapped me. It hurt like hell, but once again, I dared not show this. My eyes watered but I opened them wider so the tears would quickly evaporate and so that no one, especially Roy or Coach Kennedy, would notice. By the stinging on my cheek, I could tell the blood was rushing to it in the shape of Roy's handprint. Despite all of this, I held steady, calling upon a reserve of toughness I didn't know I had. After the initial shock at the speed with which I suddenly went from being the slapper to the slappee, another realization dawned on me. I had survived it! I was still standing across from Roy, Coach Kennedy's voice in the background saying, "That's better. Now that you've got the idea Farmer, it's your turn again."

This time I was ready. I held nothing back, nor did Roy. For the next minute or so, we took turns, along with the rest of the paired players, exchanging slaps. Then the coach told us to put our helmets on and led us out onto the practice field.

Although my face was sore and deep inside I felt like curling up and crying, another feeling was surfacing, one of pride and toughness. I had passed the first test. I was proud of myself! Somehow I had slipped over into another dimension, one that separated me from my childhood. I felt a strange mixture of loss and pride. This experience supported what I had already gathered to be true: being a man means you do not show your feelings.

Although I already had a good start at denying and holding in my feelings, the further I went into manhood, the more tests I came to, the more I knew that I dare not be emotionally vulnerable, that I could not let anyone in on my feelings. These and subsequent trials and passages helped me develop a lot of self-control, hardening me so that I could withstand pain and not let fear get in the way of action, but the cost was heavy. Unknowingly I buried my emotions more and more deeply, behind a persona based on toughness. The cost of this further woundedness was that I remained an emotional cripple, without much of a clue as to how to feel or how to be, and certainly with no idea of how to act in a relationship with others.

Exercise 5: Your Initiation Ritual

Think back to an initiation rite in which you participated when you were an adolescent or young man. What did it consist of? Did it take you away from mother? Did your father support it? What was the ordeal you had to go through? How did you feel inside? What did you show on the outside? What lessons did you learn from your experience? How did you feel about the other boys involved? Did the world look different once you had gone through the ritual? If you didn't go through an initiation ritual, how do you feel about that? Write this in your journal with as much detail as possible, and as you do be aware of what you feel. When you've completed the writing, tell your story to another man or to your men's group.

Derek described his ritual of initiation, one that he and a couple of friends created: "Tim and Terry and I started our own club. We were all about eleven years old. Tim had a treehouse in his backyard, so that's what we used as our clubhouse. It was just a flat board at first, so we took an old cardboard box that a refrigerator had come in and that was the house part.

We decided to become blood brothers, all three of us. We decided not to let any girls in the clubhouse. Tim stole some cigars from his grandfather, and we all got together one afternoon, made up a password, smoked the cigars, then took out a knife and cut our thumbs. I was scared. I kept thinking somebody's going to catch us smoking. When it was my time to cut myself, I didn't want them to see me squirm, so I took a deep breath and just did it. It wasn't that hard. Then we shared our blood—this was way before it was risky to do so—and we became blood brothers. After that we were really tight friends. It doesn't seem like it's that big of a deal, but it was then. There was something about having to go through something painful and risky, and doing it with some other guys that made it real important at the time."

This is an initiation ritual created by peers, without the guidance of older men. It suggests how powerful the need is for rituals to mark these important passages.

A culturally sanctioned ritual in Judaism is the Bar Mitzvah, a ceremony performed to mark a boy's thirteenth birthday. Barry writes about his experience:

"I'm not sure that I changed much inside, but there was a noticeable difference in the way other people treated me. It was exciting, the first time being at the center of attention—and other people started treating me like an adult. I could understand some Hebrew—I could read it by age thirteen, and forgot it by age fourteen—so I could understand quite a bit of the ceremony. But there was so much ritual, so much of it repetitive, that it was more a matter of absorbing a lot of it.

"It wasn't so much a move away from my mother into the

world of men—maybe just a bit—but more like a beginning, a
first step in striking out on my own. It wasn't a huge break. I
certainly don't look at my life as pre–Bar Mitzvah and post–Bar
Mitzvah, but I did start seeing for the first time that I could be
on my own. I'm sure that in the past this type of ritual actually
did open the doors into manhood. But these days, at 13 years
old you're still a child in many ways."

Barry's description suggests how this ritual, though rich in
ceremony and tradition, like many others, has become a pale
representation of one that more clearly marks the passage into
manhood.

OUT OF BALANCE

As I've noted, some of the attributes acquired through this
training to be a "real man" are invaluable. In fact, when we
do not limit ourselves to these attributes alone, they provide
a distinct expression of maleness into any environment. It becomes more a question of balancing these traits with an ac-
cessibility to our feelings and receptivity. In "A New Vision
of Masculinity" in *New Men, New Minds*, Cooper Thompson
says,

> Traditional definitions of masculinity include attributes
> such as independence, pride, resiliency, self-control, and
> physical strength. This is precisely the image of the
> Marlboro man, and to some extent, these are desirable
> attributes for boys and girls. But masculinity goes be-
> yond these qualities to stress competitiveness, tough-
> ness, aggressiveness, and power

When these attributes are not balanced with an ability to
be emotionally open and vulnerable, and leavened with a
healthy respect for others, they can be dangerous. One danger
is that a man can use this aggressiveness and his power to in-

timidate and manipulate others, without regard for their feelings. When a man isn't in touch with his own feelings, it's nearly impossible for him to empathize with anyone else's. Carried to the extreme, a man could blindly act out his inner rage on others and end up hurting them with his violence. Another pitfall, if a man emphasizes these characteristics at the cost of his emotional life, is that he will cut himself off from others, withdrawing and becoming distant in order to maintain control. Overdeveloping these attributes without developing an inner life can cause a man to wither and slowly die on the inside.

"I'm fifty-two years old," Tim pronounced with a sigh of resignation. "My marriage isn't going so well, I'm sick and tired of my job, and I can't seem to get ahead in the money game." Tim quit his drinking four months before and had been attending AA meetings regularly. He had come in for counseling with complaints of depression. "What really strikes me is just how alone I feel. I really notice it now that I'm no longer drinking. The other day after work I felt such a strong urge to drink, I thought, 'maybe just a margarita,' but I just didn't want to do what I'd always done. Instead I came home, sat down on the couch, and just started crying. The tears wouldn't stop, and I don't usually cry. My wife, Maggie, didn't know what to say— she's not used to this, I'm sure. I hardly slept at all that night. It's like there's a big empty space inside me." Tim has hit a point in his life where it no longer works to keep his feelings shut down.

This happens to many of us. Often, before a man can confront the pain of his woundedness he must reach a point of emptiness where he recognizes that all his old ways of covering up no longer work. One of the ways a man can cover up his fear, hurt, anger, sadness, and happiness—whatever life energy remains—is with some sort of addictive behavior.

The Addiction Paradox

When I use the term *addiction* or *addictive behavior* I'm not necessarily referring only to what most people typically think of as
hard-core addictions. I'm referring to any process that has control over your life, one that you obsess about and indulge in
compulsively and with progressively greater frequency, and one
in which you find yourself lying, denying, and covering up. If
you hide those ice cream cartons at the bottom of the trash so
no one will notice, then you've got an addiction to ice cream.
If you find yourself watching television with increasing frequency to occupy your attention, then you are watching television addictively.

There are two types of addictions. First, there are *substance*
addictions. These are anything that you ingest, including alcohol, drugs, food, or tobacco. Alcohol and drugs, the chemical
addictions, are especially problematic because they very directly
alter the body's biochemistry and in many instances can prove
physiologically addictive. A second type of addiction is called
a *process* addiction. This is any activity that, while it does not
directly alter a person's biochemistry, does alter mood and works
to repress difficult feelings—in other words, any process that
generally numbs you out. Some examples are work, sex, relationships, masturbation, gambling, television, and exercise. Although all of these are quite normal activities, any of them can
be used addictively.

Whether substance or process, what's important to understand is how a person develops and maintains an addiction.
While there are always other factors involved, one of the primary determinants is this difficulty in dealing with feelings to
which, as men, we are particularly subject. The addiction then
goes on to maintain an emotional numbness that prevents us
from learning how to open up our feelings and learn to deal
with, and express them, more effectively.

At the root of any addictive behavior is an inability to
manage feelings, coupled with a tendency toward low self-
esteem. Even more deeply at the root of addiction is a spiritual

bankruptcy, a sense of emptiness and disconnectedness. When we are troubled by disturbing feelings about which we have little knowledge and perhaps even less experience in dealing with effectively, we learn very quickly to turn to something external to ease our pain and discomfort. We look to alcohol, television, food—anything that works to keep us from feeling what we don't want to feel. We can then become habituated to it if we find that it helps us to maintain a psychic numbness while at the same time giving us a charge and/or an escape from unpleasant and unmanageable feelings.

Work addiction, a common one for men, is one in which work is used in an attempt to fulfill all of man's needs. By working compulsively a man can numb himself to unwelcome feelings such as vulnerability, anger, or hurt, and still feel the rush of power and accomplishment that comes from being so closely identified and enmeshed with his actions.

Sandy is just starting to question the motives behind his ninety-hour-plus work weeks for the past ten years. "I quit my old job in part because I reached a plateau, but also because my wife threatened to leave me if I didn't do something about cutting my hours. I've hardly known my two sons, and they've both started school now. The thing is, a few months ago I started on this new job, and I can feel how I want to be working more and more. Part of why I want to do that is so I can make some more money; it takes a lot of money to raise a family these days. But I think I might be attracted to more hours because I don't know what to do at home, where I feel restless and don't know what to do with myself. Meg has gotten used to dealing with the children on her own. I try to help out, but she'll say something and I'll feel like I'm interfering. I get really pissed off at her, but I know that a lot of it is just the tension of my being home. Last week for the first time I took some work home with me for the weekend, something I swore I'd never do. I'm really torn. I feel like I want to be with Meg and the children, yet I feel tugged at by my need to do a good job. I don't see a solution yet."

Sandy obviously feels trapped between his need to be the

provider for his family and his needs for closeness and intimacy. He has had very little experience with closeness growing up in his own family. While his work is important, as it is for most men, it has become an overriding excuse for avoiding issues of intimacy for which he is ill prepared.

When something becomes addictive, we turn to it whenever there is stress or we've become upset. Much of our life is centered on and planned around the next "fix," whether it be work, sex, a relationship, alcohol, television, or any other substance or activity. If you find that a good deal of your thoughts are obsessively fixated on that substance or activity, and that you give in to the obsession by acting it out, then you have an addiction. Ultimately it can become the focal point for much of your life.

A few years ago my girl friend Ann Marie and I broke up. We had been steady lovers for just under a year, and I had become consumed with her, thinking about her when she wasn't with me and eagerly awaiting our next opportunity to be together. I put all of my needs into that relationship. My work suffered, my other friendships suffered—everything else took a backseat. Up until I started seeing her I had been recovering from my divorce, which was less than a year old when I met her. I had been crying, getting angry, writing regularly in my journal, and working hard in therapy to keep my feelings moving and to let go of my former wife.

When Ann Marie came along, she became my fix. I could feel exhilarated with her. Sex with her became a way to feel something, to temporarily awaken the deadness that I felt inside, and, as with most addictions, to fill the emptiness, the yearning for comfort and love—at least for a moment. In the meantime, my other feelings got more and more stuck and I became oblivious to them. As long as I was addictively involved with someone I didn't have to deal with my grief or my pain—not only the pain that still lingered from the divorce, but the pain of unmet needs and unexpressed emotions that had been with me most of my life. Ann Marie and I laughed and played and had sex a lot, and I clung to her as though Velcro was holding my heart to hers.

One day she announced that she wanted to "start dating other men." She had been rehearsing for a dance performance and I knew that she was attracted to one of the fellows in the show. Much of the anger and tears that had been sidetracked during the course of our relationship came out during the next few weeks. My behavior became erratic, going from thinking that I could continue seeing her while she slept with another man to feeling outraged and wanting to do some damage to her car or to her, to make her hurt like I did. The extent of my acting out was to rage at her upon occasion.

Three days after Ann Marie's announcement, I knew she was with "him." I could not stop fantasizing that they were engaged in hot, passionate sex and continued to torture myself with images of the two of them together. I happened to know that her new boyfriend lived in a nearby city, less than fifteen minutes away, although I didn't know his precise address. I deduced from what information I had that he lived in one section of this city that covered only a few square blocks. Lying awake at midnight, feeling my loneliness, my pain, and my rage, I began to plot how I could probably drive around this section of town and look for Ann Marie's car. I wasn't sure what I would do when I found it, but the more I thought about it, the more I felt compelled to act.

I got up, got dressed, and hopped into my van. Through the entire time I carried on a dialogue with myself, sometimes out loud, sometimes just in my head. It was a dialogue between the rational part of me and the compulsive, addictive, needy part of me. It went something like this:

"What the hell are you doing out here driving around at midnight? What are you going to do if you do find her? This makes absolutely no sense at all!"

"I know that! Just shut up and let me drive! I've *got* to find her! I can't stand it anymore! I have to see this guy! I have to know!"

"Oh, so you're going to find her car, run in on them, and beat them up? You know you won't do that."

"I don't know what I'll do! I just have to find them!"

And so the internal conversation proceeded for the hour that I drove around the city trying to locate her car. It was crazy. I drove up and down the blocks within the radius where I thought he lived, but to no avail. I finally surrendered to the fact that I had either miscalculated where he lived or that there was some other explanation for why I hadn't found them. Afterward I felt embarrassed and angry at myself, and vowed that I would never behave this way again. It was my first glimmering that maybe, just maybe, I was addicted to her. It was a sobering experience.

Realizing that it was futile to try to control the outcome with Ann Marie, I agonized for the next several days about what to do next. We did see each other once during this time, but I found it was just too painful. It wasn't the same. I knew I had to end the relationship and cut off all contact—for my own healing. As painful as it was to do that, it would have been even more painful to continue seeing her. And yet all through my abstinence, as irrational as it was, I still held out a glimmer of hope that someday we could be together and live happily ever after.

As time went on it became more apparent that this was pure fantasy—it was simply not going to happen. As I let go of the notion that someday we might kiss and make up, I began to feel my grief. Not only the grief of losing her, but all the hurt and pain over the losses I had experienced following my divorce. For several weeks, I spent many hours in my room, pounding my bed with my fist, with a big box of Kleenex and my trusty journal at my side. As long as I had been addictively involved with Ann Marie, I didn't have to experience my feelings of loss and isolation. Instead, I would try to give myself a "fix" whenever I started feeling anything resembling pain or upset.

It was through grieving my losses that I began to reverse the emotional numbing that had been with me most of my life.

This is often how many of us are introduced to our healing—by a major life upset that wounds us to such an extent that we can no longer avoiding feeling it. We may find ourselves using some- thing addictively to try to cover up our painful feelings.

If you think you may be addicted, seek professional help and/or look for a 12-step program that addresses your particular addiction. There are a multitude of 12-step programs modeled after the highly successful Alcoholics Anonymous. There are also Codependents Anonymous, Adult Children of Alcoholics, Co- caine Anonymous, Sexual Compulsives Anonymous, and Over- eaters Anonymous, to name a few. Calling the local chapter of Alcoholics Anonymous (AA) will give you some leads as to where to find other groups that may be more appropriate for you. I would suggest that whatever meeting you find, you attend at least six sessions before deciding whether to continue.

Whatever your method of keeping your feelings under cover, there are some things you can do to open yourself up. That's where we will look next.

4

A Man and His Feelings: Opening Up

By the time I was thirty-five years old and in a second marriage that was beginning to fall apart, after years of being shut down emotionally and spiritually, of using various addictions to stave off these unfamiliar and uncomfortable feelings, I was ripe for a change. I then had two children, and although I loved them dearly, I felt ill prepared for fathering. I felt myself growing more and more isolated. Smoking two packs of cigarettes a day, marijuana whenever I could get some, and on occasion snorting cocaine, I was feeling totally inadequate as a provider, earning only a marginal income.

We were in debt up to our ears, in good part because I had several pieces of plastic that promised I could enjoy now and pay later. I takes no financial wizard to see that if you buy something for $1000 and pay it off at $30 per month with a good chunk of that going toward interest, and you keep buying a lot of somethings with the total cost of all these somethings being more than you earn, eventually this is going to catch up to you. I had considered bankruptcy seriously at least twice, but up until then had bowed out because of the shame and humiliation that I attached to it. Besides, bankruptcy would mean giving up. I was desperate, yet I concealed this desperation behind my isolation and kept up a stone face. I walled everyone off, including the woman I lived with and who loved me, for fear that they would see how helpless I felt. I was sinking fast. I didn't know where to turn, so instead I just got more depressed and withdrawn. In Alcoholics Anonymous, the wisdom is that the alcoholic may often have to "bottom out" before coming to the realization of his disease. This period of time was certainly my bottoming-out. It seems that many of us find our openings in a crisis.

At that time I participated in an encounter training, a very intense, five-day course wherein I explored and examined my life in great detail through lectures and various exercises. Through my experience in these exercises I discovered some of the habitual routines and masks that I used to operate with in the world—and learned how to drop them.

For the first three days of training, I began to see just how much I remained hidden and closed up. It was very painful, but as usual I shared very little of my experience with anyone else. By the fourth day I was feeling weary, but at the same time completely intrigued by what was happening inside me and to others around me. People were coming alive, making direct eye contact, laughing, smiling, hugging others. I liked the energy that surrounded me, but as was so often true in my life, I felt that I wasn't a part of it. I knew something was beginning to happen inside me, but I wasn't sure what it was or what to do with it. As intimidating as it was, I also felt compelled to push further and continue to participate 100 percent in the course.

It was late afternoon of the fourth day. In the large group the facilitator instructed us to find a partner, someone we didn't necessarily like but who we thought would be really tough with us. My eyes immediately went to a woman I considered was an absolute bitch. Strangely enough, she was also looking straight at me. I have no idea what she was thinking about me. We moved toward each other and paired up, knees to knees. We introduced ourselves and I found out her name was Barbara. There was no further comment or conversation as we waited apprehensively, avoiding each other's eyes, for further instructions.

The directions were simple enough. One of us was to ask the other repeatedly, "What do you want?" as the other answered. The partner asking the question was to ask it as if drilling for oil, to shout the question if necessary. We were not to let up until the facilitator told us to stop. Little did I know that this redundant line of inquiry would go on for several minutes each way. We were to maintain eye contact throughout the exercise. With the instructions to choose who would be drilled first, I muttered something to her about my going first and she agreed. Although we were already close, she leaned toward me, planted her feet, and put her hands on her knees, elbows high, waiting for the starting gun. When the facilitator said, "Go!" she screamed at me—"WHAT DO YOU WANT?!"—while all around me in this gymnasium-sized room there were others shouting the same at their partners. The cacophony was deafening, yet in spite of it, I could clearly hear Barbara's question.

At first I tried to get cute, joking it away. "A new car."

"WHAT DO YOU WANT?!"

"A house by the ocean."

"WHAT DO YOU WANT?!"

"More money."

"WHAT DO YOU WANT?!"

"Three square meals and a place to flop."

Barbara didn't budge, nor did she even crack a smile at my poor attempts at lightening the situation. I had chosen wisely. As I went through my initial nervousness and judgments about the absurdity of the exercise, a door began to open just a tiny bit. Barbara was relentless.

"WHAT DO YOU WANT?!"

"I want my children to be happy."

"WHAT DO YOU WANT?!"

"I want to be happy."

"WHAT DO YOU WANT?!"

"I want to enjoy my work."

"WHAT DO YOU WANT?!"

"I want to clear up all my debts."

"WHAT DO YOU WANT?!"

"I want to feel my feelings."

This was getting serious. In spite of all the shouting going on around me, I stayed very focused on Barbara's questioning. I became aware of an emotional surge inside me as the door

opened a little bit further. I could feel a bolt of pain shoot
upward from my genitals and belly into my face. Tears started
streaming down as I felt the grief of years of emotional suppression and isolation. Then came the response that took me over
the edge.

"WHAT DO YOU WANT?!"

"I want to be loved."

Barbara softened. "What do you want?"!

"I want to be loved, and I want to love!"

"What do you want?"

"I WANT TO BE LOVED! I WANT TO LOVE! OH,
GOD, I WANT TO BE LOVED!"

All my masks that had covered this one simple need were
ripped away. I was crying, smiling, laughing, and bubbling with
exuberance all at the same time. I was alive, and I could feel
it! Barbara was smiling and laughing as well, affected by the
pure and innocent delight of my response. The exercise continued in this way for a while longer, but I had gone beyond the
exercise to a place where grief and ecstasy were one, surging
forward in a raw expression of vital feeling and need.

Barbara and I switched roles. A similar experience happened for her, and it was quite moving. I sensed as I did my
part that something in me had lifted, and I was prepared to let
the world know that it had. When we finished, the facilitator
instructed us to lie down. As we did, he voiced a soothing
meditation that seemed to deepen the experience. I was so excited I was bursting in spite of the meditation. Then he went
on to say, "In a few moments I'm going to ask you to open
your eyes. When you do so, go with your partner on the break,
and talk with each other about what happened for you. Okay,
open your eyes, get with your partner, and talk with them on
the break."

I sat up gradually, looked eagerly to Barbara, excitedly prepared to share with her my revelation. She looked squarely at
me and very matter-of-factly said, "I'm going to go with my
husband."

Her words were like a knife cutting from my belly to my

heart. I felt so open and raw, so newly vulnerable that I was totally shocked by her sudden withdrawal. I felt my connection with her being ripped away. I needed her desperately, as she was the first person to witness my coming out, what I was to later term my "spiritual birthday." But instead, I said reflexively, "Sure," and went into my I-can-handle-it routine. She trotted off to be with her husband. Instead of being angry with her, I felt ashamed of myself for even having the need, for daring to open myself up with someone. Feeling completely shattered on the inside, I got up and sauntered slowly out to the large sitting room where several of the other participants had already gathered. There I spotted a large overstuffed chair, sat down, somewhat shakily pulled out a cigarette, and lit up.

Soon the room was filled with many of those from the class. Everyone was with his or her partner, and all were talking excitedly and animatedly about their experiences. I gathered from some of the conversations I tuned into that for many the exercise had been as significant a revelation as it had been for me. Looking about and seeing that everyone was with someone else made me feel even more alone. It felt as if there was a huge spotlight singling me out as the only one in the room without a partner. My insides felt raw and my mind was scrambled. Everything that I had come to believe about myself seemed wrong. Yet through it all I steeled my feelings as I had done for so many years, using everything in my power to keep it together. It is so typical of us as men to deny our vulnerability and our need and instead to "tough it out."

At that point one of the course assistants spotted me, came over to me, and put her hand on my forearm. My forearm burned where she touched me. My longing to be loved and cared for, which I'd felt my whole life but had buried in denial, had reawakened. I ached to satisfy it at that moment, yet was at the same time shrunken in terror to be feeling something so intensely. So I did my best to maintain my cool as the smoke from my cigarette swirled about my head. She looked at me directly and said, "Are you okay?" I ached inside to tell her of my dilemma, fantasized curling up in her arms and letting the sobs that were choked down in my gut come out in their full glory. I yearned to tell her of my astounding discovery, that it was basically very simple—I just wanted to be loved and to love! Instead, my years of habit took over, and in response to her very sincere inquiry, I replied, "I'm fine," with all the conviction of a cat who had been caught with its paw in the goldfish bowl. She gave me a look that said she wasn't convinced, but respected my apparent need to be alone.

After the break, we all gathered for another session, this one a lecture. I have to this day no idea what was going on during the lecture, or how long it lasted. I was in a trance the entire time, my whole belief system crumbling inside me. Once the lecture ended, however, I instinctively knew I needed to act. I walked directly to one of the men from the smaller group that I was in and grabbed him by the arm. Somehow I knew that he was a man I needed to connect with. As I got hold of him I started babbling away about my discovery, evidently making some sense. He commented that I had seemed very aloof when I first walked into the course, and was glad that I had come down from my tower.

From that point on the rest of the course was a breeze. After it was all over, much of what I had experienced there carried over into my daily life. My eyes were actually much more open, as were my emotions. I felt happy to be alive. I could look people in the eyes and really see them. I experienced a closeness with others, particularly my wife and children, that I had never remembered feeling before in my entire life. When I was sad, scared, happy, angry, or loving, I could really *feel* these emotions. I experienced an increased sense of personal responsibility, a feeling that I could do something about my present situation and no longer needed to feel victimized by my circumstances. Something had definitely shifted inside me. Remaining emotionally distant and numb was no longer appealing. I liked this new state of being alive and awake.

Yet waking up one time does not in itself constitute a transformation. I wish I could say this experience of opening immediately helped me save my marriage, clear myself of debt, make lots more money, and stop drugs altogether, but it didn't. However, it did change my life. It marked a beginning for me of slowly but steadily cleaning up my life, of making a commitment to staying awake rather than sleeping. It was the first time I began to take full responsibility for my choices, and to really *feel* my emotions rather than blocking them out.

Perhaps, as it did for me, it took a crisis in your life to lead you into feeling your emotions. Perhaps it has been a more gradual awareness that something was missing. Whatever the path that has led you here, you have the opportunity now to go into the uncharted territory of emotions. Although I can't provide you with a complete map of the territory, in this chapter I can give you some guidelines and suggestions for your travels.

Throughout I offer ideas and exercises—some fairly mild, some quite challenging—that I have used myself, and used with my friends and my clients to open up and experience emotions. These can help you expand your capacity to feel and express the entire range of your emotions as well as be more aware of what it is you are feeling.

One note: Although most of these ideas and exercises can be used alone, I recommend doing some of them with other men. If you are a member of a men's group or if you start one after reading this book, then use them in the group. It will be risky, challenging, and even more rewarding to work with this opening-up emotionally with other men.

A MAN AND HIS FEELINGS

I remember a scene in *Godfather III* where Michael Corleone, especially angry at his ex-wife, was confronting a number of problems in his life. His eyes widened, the veins in his neck bulged, and he was going into a black rage, pacing back and forth and shouting at her, "WE MUST BE REASONABLE!" His anguished cry is an absurd attempt to deny his feelings, yet reflects what many of us try to do with our emotions. I know that when I was married to my second wife I thought she had a major problem if being so emotional, when in truth my rigidity was based on my own ingrained fear of emotions. I was afraid a lot of the time, although I wasn't necessarily conscious of it. My way of acting on the feeling of fear was to withdraw and stay distant.

A key to learning to experience and express your feelings more readily is to practice awareness. Awareness means paying attention and, with emotions, learning specifically to pay attention to what's going on in your body. Noticing physical sensations, such as where you feel tense, constricted, or flushed, can give you clues as to what you are feeling emotionally. Learning to associate these physical sensations with particular emotions starts with your willingness to pay closer attention and become more aware of these sensations.

Awareness directly contradicts everything you've learned along the way that told you it was better to keep your feelings to yourself or to shut down and stay shut down. The more you practice staying awake, alert, and aware, the more you will open the way to fully acknowledging your emotions. Addictions, particularly chemical addictions of any sort, will block you from feeling. That's why we use them—to *not* feel. To awaken your emotions completely, it is important to stop using the addictive substance to keep yourself numb.

Luke had been sober for six months, attending Alcoholics Anonymous regularly, and working hard to turn his life around. He described how he started becoming aware of his emotions: "I had stopped drinking after one binge where I had a blackout. I knew at that point I had to do something about it, and it was rough. I was keeping busy, going to [AA] meetings so I wouldn't have to think much about what was going on. One evening a few weeks after I'd quit I was at home and Gail was gone. I saw a picture in a magazine of this little boy and I just started crying and crying and couldn't stop. Then it hit me. This was a feeling! I kept saying over and over, 'This is a feeling! This is a feeling!' Even though it was painful, I was laughing because it seemed so simple at the time."

Another key element is to understand the difference between feeling and doing. To feel something, whether it be anger, fear, or any other emotion does not mean you have to act on that feeling. As men we are especially oriented toward action, to do something about a feeling, to treat it as a problem to be solved. Feelings can provide extremely valuable information to help you understand yourself or come to a decision, yet, I repeat, having a feeling does not mean you must act on it. You can simply feel it, allowing the feeling to wash over you. In some instances it is very important to act on your feelings, such as acting on fear when there is a tangible danger. When you are driving in your car and you suddenly see someone swerving into your lane, your fear reaction is necessary for you to take appropriate action. If action is called for, you can act in spite of your fear or your anger. On the other hand, if you feel like hitting someone in the face it would typically not work to act out that urge. For the vast majority of feelings you can simply notice them, feel them—without having to deny them or act them out impulsively.

When you deny and repress your emotions, depression results. What we call depression is the result of remaining emotionally numb and shut down much of your life. It originates in the wounds you received in childhood, when you were traumatized by physical, emotional, or sexual abuse. Your instinctual reaction was to shut down your feelings. I was depressed for much of my adult life and didn't even know it. I assumed that it was normal to go around psychically numb and emotionally unavailable. After all, this is how I saw most men living their daily lives.

ENERGY IN MOTION

Emotions are pure energy. In fact, we could say that emotion is energy in motion, e-motion. Whatever the emotion, it starts as pure energy, is experienced as a sensation in the body, then either moves upward and outward into expression of some sort, is quietly felt and experienced, or else gets blocked and stalled somewhere in the body. For instance, at the end of the day, have you ever felt tension in your neck and shoulders that has no discernible cause? Do you notice your diaphragm area being particularly tight? Do you keep your jaw tensed, or grind your teeth? Very likely this is the anger, fear, and/or pain that you have experienced but suppressed. As Einstein said, energy can never be created or destroyed, but only transmuted, either into another form of energy or into denser material called matter. Another consequence of continually repressing and suppressing this energy, whether it be the energy of anger, pain, fear, or sadness, is that your immune system gets zapped and drained; your body's natural ability to ward off disease thereby becomes impaired. The energy that lies trapped in the body can then contribute to the disease process. For instance, when you hold tension in your stomach, it may result in an upset stomach. If this is chronic, the excess acid that is secreted when your stomach is upset could contribute to an ulcer.

YOUR BODY'S PART

It's sad but true that we men have learned to ignore our bodies. Sure, you may run, work out at the gym, ride your bicycle in pursuit of a healthy body, and if so, you are to be commended. However, what we have learned to ignore is the emotions that are seated in our bodies, particularly those that originate in the middle third of our bodies—the torso. It has been culturally sanctioned that men operate from our gonads and from our heads, but not from our gut and our heart. It's okay for men to intellectualize and be sexual, but not to be tender, open, or vulnerable. Any numbness that we have is particularly acute in this middle section.

What's required is to start paying regular attention to what is going on inside your body. Do the following exercise at least two times a week for the next twenty-one days as a way of becoming more aware of your body.

Exercise 6: Body Awareness

To do this exercise either have someone you trust record it on a cassette or do so yourself. Read it slowly, and be sure to pause for a few moments between each sentence. When you're ready, find a comfortable chair to sit on. Sit up rather than lying down so you have less of a chance of going to sleep. Notice that the exercise is broken into three parts. Record the entire exercise, but leave a lengthier pause between each step so you can stop the cassette either after step one or step two, depending on how far you choose to go. Close your eyes, focus on your breathing, turn on the cassette, then proceed:

STEP 1: Start by noticing your breathing. Is it steady? Labored? Shallow? Take a slow, deep breath, releasing it very slowly. Do this again. Let your breathing return to a more natural rhythm. Note the rise and fall of your chest. Slowly scan your body from head to foot. What parts of your body are carrying tension? What parts are relaxed? Are there any areas that feel numb? Notice parts of your head where there is some strain. Perhaps your forehead. Your eyes. What about your jaw? No need to do anything, simply be aware. Sometimes becoming aware of tension in specific points in your body is enough to relax them.

Continue moving your attention gradually, steadily down your body. Notice your neck, then shoulders. Is there tension in your shoulders? Next, notice your arms, then your chest. Take a deep, slow breath and feel how your chest expands. Be aware of your hands and your fingers. Next, be aware of your lower back, where it touches the surface upon which you're sitting. Notice your stomach. Is there tension in your diaphragm area? Numbness? If so, breathe it out, let it relax.

Continue down your body. Notice your buttocks, where they touch the surface you're sitting on. Be aware of your anus. Notice your penis, testicles, scrotum, and how it feels to bring your attention so directly to your genitals. Then move your attention to your thighs, both front and back. Next, notice your knees. Then move your attention to your shins, calves. Now to your feet. The tops, then the bottoms, then your toes. Be aware of any tension or numbness that remains. Once again, take a slow deep breath, and feel all the areas of your body that are relaxed. . . .

(PAUSE)

STEP 2: Now as you continue to relax and breathe deeply and slowly, take both of your hands and slowly lift them to your face, placing your fingers lightly on your forehead. Lightly move your fingers across your forehead, around your temples, under your eyes, and to other areas of your face. Do so gently and slowly, paying close attention to the sensation in your hands and your face. Touch your ears, hair, jaw, and mouth. Notice any feelings that surface. Next, take your hands slowly away from your face as you take a deep breath. Now slowly explore your hands and arms. First use your right hand to explore your left hand and arm, then vice versa. Feel the shape of your hand, fingers, wrist, and arm. Use different pressures, different strokes. Notice both the touching and the being touched.

When this is completed, relax one of your arms and put one of your hands over your chest and heart. Hold your hand steady for a few moments and notice any sensations or feelings. Next, move your hand downward to your solar plexus and rest it there for a few moments. Be aware of any tension or numbness there. Notice how it feels to rest your hand there. Now, move your hand down to cover the area between your navel and your genitals. Once again, notice how this feels. Hold it there for the next few moments, feel the light pressure of your hand. Be aware throughout of any emotions that this touching stirs up. Take a slow, deep breath and relax your hand at your side.

(PAUSE)

STEP 3: Take one of your arms and slowly lift it to shoulder height while silently saying to yourself, "My arm is moving." Carefully note what muscles in your arm, back, shoulders, it takes to move your arm. Notice the slight shifts in your muscles as you raise your arm. Next, lower it slowly, as you continue paying attention to your muscle movements.

Once it is at rest, pause for a few moments. Now raise it slowly once again, this time thinking, "I am moving my arm." Once again, notice the movements in your muscles. Especially note the subtle difference in where your attention is centered this way. Lower your arm slowly, gently, letting your entire body relax completely.

Now return your attention to your breathing. Take a slow, deep breath and release it very slowly. Do this again. Notice the contrast between the tension and the relaxation as you breathe in, and as you breathe out. Open your eyes and reorient yourself to the room you are in by looking around and listening to any sounds you notice.

Harold described what happened when he tried this exercise for the first time: "I liked it. At first I felt a little silly, like I kept wondering, 'What's the point?' The part where you raise your arm and say, 'I'm moving my arm,' and then 'My arm is moving,' now that was something else. I could really feel a difference in the two. When I was thinking, 'My arm is moving,' I felt more detached somehow, but at the same time very aware of the sensation of my arm moving. When I thought, 'I'm moving my arm,' I felt very much in charge of doing it. I also noticed how much tension I carry in my shoulders. It's like I go around with my shoulders covering my ears."

GRIEVING AS THE DOORWAY

For a man to heal his wounds, he must learn how to grieve. In the chapter entitled "Fathers and Sons," I described how important it was in healing the father wound to grieve the loss of the father you never had. There are many other losses in our lives that we as men have learned to ignore. These losses are both tangible and abstract. Perhaps you lost someone you cared about through death or their moving away, or perhaps you experienced the loss of status due to a career demotion. Perhaps there are other childhood losses that you remember, such as having changed schools or losing a favorite pet. No matter what it is, if you feel in any way that you have lost something, then you have, and it's best to grieve it.

Such losses as the one I described in the first chapter, where I recalled how I had been taken off the baseball team, may seem inconsequential or trivial. Yet when these kinds of experiences go unacknowledged and aren't addressed at the time they happen—as is often the case with childhood events, then there still may be some feelings trapped inside. It doesn't matter how long it's been since the loss; or even how many times you've grieved about it before, at any time you may begin thinking about it and feel some renewed grief over it.

In our culture there haven't been a lot of allowances for the grief work that inevitably accompanies a loss. Most businesses will give you a paltry two or three days off in the event of a death in the family, and most people will expect you to be over your grieving within a few short weeks. While some losses may indeed be grieved in fairly short order, most major losses require a minimum of two or three years of active grieving. During that time you will be feeling a lot of anger and sadness, and you may be doing a lot of crying. It may be intermittent or it may be a steady stream. The length of the grieving process depends on the individual. Everyone's pattern is different.

Being a man in this culture has made it doubly difficult because of our restrictions on emotional expression. If you follow a more traditional male patterning, then you will tend to wall off and deny your grief, only to have it weigh you down in the form of a depression. There is far more support for denial than there is for real, genuine feelings. Even the most well-intentioned friends will make statements such as, "Just put the past behind you," or "It was meant to be," in response to your self-disclosure; these are examples of how grieving is often met with a "just put on a happy face" mentality that is so typical of our culture. Most people do not want to feel their grief intensely because it doesn't always look very pretty; it certainly isn't neat and tidy. If someone were to truly respond, to sincerely empathize with another's pain and grief, he would have to feel his own pain, and that is usually unacceptable, especially for men.

A few weeks before my mother died, I had a conversation with my dad about grieving. She had been bedridden for well over a year, and was gradually slipping away. At one point when I was visiting, he confided that he thought the end was near, that she had "had another one of her mini-strokes," and could go at any time. I went into the bedroom where she was and could immediately see that she had worsened. After a visit with her, I returned to sit at the kitchen table with my father to be with him. He was obviously in a lot of pain and was frightened.

"She has gotten worse, Dad," I said.

He looked up from the tabletop where his gaze had been directed and I could see that his eyes were getting misty. "Yeah, I know. She's getting to where she can hardly talk. It's not going to be long now." Hunched over in his chair, he slowly stubbed out the cigarette he had been smoking. Suddenly he looked very old. "I'm going to miss the old gal. We've been together forty-four years. That's a pretty long time to be with any one person."

At this point my dad's voice started cracking and his tears started trickling down his face. As if he'd caught himself, he sat up, dabbed at his eyes, and said, "I guess I'm acting like a baby."

That statement caught me by surprise. I was torn up with my own grief and at the same time I felt annoyed with him. I looked at him and said, "Dad! You've been with this woman for over forty years and you may lose her at any time. This isn't about being a baby, it's about grieving, plain and simple. You've got to claim your grief! It's a natural part of healing from something like this. And I'm glad you're letting me in on this."

He heard me.

Although there is no set way to do your grieving, most likely it will be a combination of angry and sad feelings. When you do the following exercises, let yourself be a bit uncomfortable by feeling any grief you have more strongly than you would usually feel it.

Exercise 7: Remembering Your Grief

Think back on a time in your life when you experienced a loss. It might be something from childhood, adolescence, or something more recent. How old were you? Who else was involved? Where were you when this took place? What were your feelings at the time? What did you do with your feelings? Did you get angry? Cry? Was there anyone else you shared them with? How would you have liked to handle the loss? What do you feel as you think of it now?

Now write about this experience in as much detail as possible in your journal.

Victor wrote about when his grandfather died: "I was really close to my grandfather, and I know I was his favorite grandchild. I was about eight years old, and I remember the day my mom told me he had been taken to the hospital. She said he'd had a stroke, but I didn't know what that was at the time. I couldn't sleep that night, and the next morning my mom told me that Grandpa had died at the hospital. I cried and cried. After that, not a whole lot was said. I don't remember my dad ever crying, even though it was his own father who had died.

The strangest part was seeing my grandpa in the casket. That I didn't like at all. I still have a picture in my mind of how white he looked. And nobody explained anything or talked to me about what was going on. I felt very much alone throughout most of it. We went to the funeral, he went into the ground, and that was that. I didn't cry for the longest time after that. In fact, that's the last time I ever remember crying so hard. Now when I think of Grandpa, I really miss him. He was there for me in a way that my father never was."

Victor clearly has some unfinished grieving for his grandfather.

Another instance of loss is when I was about eighteen years old. I had a dog, Schroeder, named after the piano player in the "Peanuts" comic strip, who was a cross between a golden retriever and a spaniel. I got him when he was a puppy and raised him and trained him myself. He was my companion at a time in my life when I had started college, was still living at my parents' home, and didn't really have any close friends. I really loved him, and like most dogs do with their masters, he loved me unconditionally.

When he was about two years old he developed a painful skin condition. I took him to a veterinarian who, after several tests, pronounced this condition incurable and suggested that I have Schroeder "put to sleep," a euphemism that is cruel in its kind denial. He told me to think about it and let him know the next day.

That night I barely slept. The next morning, with a huge lump in my throat, I called the doctor and told him I would be bringing Schroeder in to have him injected. My parents were gone that afternoon, so I went into the backyard and had a private good-bye talk with my friend. I'm sure he also knew it was time to say good-bye. I put him in the back of my station wagon—perhaps he thought we were going for one of our walks or to the school to play fetch. His energy was quite low, so I changed my mind and had him come up to the front seat with me. In one of the longest drives I ever made, we took off to the veterinary hospital. All through the drive he kept his head on my lap—again as if he knew it was our last trip—while I stroked his ears.

Dr. Granville was ready for us. I checked in, and after a brief wait, we went into the examination room. The doctor said that I could stay if I wanted to, but I couldn't bear it. My heart literally hurt. I muttered something about sending the payment in, and the doctor in his kindness said, "Don't worry about it." I said a hurried good-bye to Dr. Granville and then looked at Schroeder. My voice a barely audible whisper, I bent close to him, looked at his sad eyes, and said, "Good-bye, Schroeder. I love you." Then I turned and walked quickly away.

As I walked out the door I could barely contain my sobbing. I went to the side of the hospital where my car was parked, looked around, quickly unlocked my car and slid in, and then I cut loose. I cried like I had never cried before, sobbing loudly as I shut the car door and started the engine. I drove up a back road to the college I was attending, found the parking lot, stopped the car in the far corner, and cried for the next several minutes. In my mind I kept seeing the look on Schroeder's face at the hospital. And now he was dead. All the logic that I could muster told me it had been the right thing to do, yet for a long time afterward, I felt guilty, as if it were my fault.

Exercise 8: Sharing Your Grief

Now for the real challenge. Take what you have written and read it to a trusted man friend or else bring it to your men's group and read it aloud. Read it slowly, pausing to notice what's going on in your body and feeling your emotions as you read it. Don't hold back. Go as far as you can with feeling what's moving emotionally. If this is hard for you, let the person you are reading it to know that it is, and that you want his support in doing so. If you are part of a men's group, this can be a group assignment—each participant writes his story out, and then takes turns reading it.

Victor read the story of his grandfather to his friend Phillip. He reports: "Even though I was a little nervous I really thought it wouldn't be that difficult. But what a surprise! Phillip was listening really close, and at one point he started getting tears in his eyes. I could feel my stomach tighten and a big, fat lump in my throat, especially as I was remembering what my grandpa looked like in the casket. I broke down and started crying, and felt really embarrassed. But Phillip reached out and put his hand on my shoulder, and I could see that he was still crying right along with me. It actually felt good to have someone there, even though I was quite self-conscious about showing my grief to him. I continued to read the story, even though my hands and voice were shaking, and I had to stop a few times."

Scott wrote an account of an earlier loss along with everyone in his men's group. He described what it was like reading it to his group: "This was hard to do. It helped that we had all done the assignment. A couple of guys read their stories and everyone in the group was really touched by them. Jeremy read the story about his mother dying when he was fifteen, and Chuck wrote about when his parents got divorced. Most of the guys were weeping, and there was a lot of compassion and a lot we could all identify with.

"I went next. I read my story about how when I was nine or ten years old and I had come home and my dog Sparky was gone. My mom told me he had run away, but I knew she was lying even though I didn't say anything to her. As I read the story, I could feel my body tensing up, particularly my jaws. I was getting angry as I read it. It still pisses me off not only that they gave my dog away, but they lied about it as well. I never did confront them about the lie. I really missed that dog, too."

Whenever you have a sense that you need to do some grief work, use your journal to stimulate your emotions. Simply write what's going on in your body and with your feelings. Free associate on paper what is happening as you experience whatever sense of loss you have. If anger becomes the dominant feeling over sadness, there are ways you can work specifically with your anger.

ANGER DOESN'T HAVE TO HURT

Most of us have an issue with anger. Anger can be quite terrifying, whether in someone else or ourselves. We all, for the
most part, learned early on that when people get angry, there's
a lot of pain. You may have come to believe that anger equals
pain and therefore tried to turn it off in yourself by staying cool
and avoiding getting angry at all costs. And you did whatever
you could to avoid having someone else get angry with you.

In attempting to sidestep anger, however, you have probably found by now that it's impossible to avoid angry feelings.
When I was growing up, anger meant a lot of chaos and unresolved emotions. I vowed that I would never get angry like my
dad or mom or brother did. Yet when I was a young man, whenever I reached a boiling point I would go into a rage and hit
walls. There were a few apartments I lived in where I had
punched actual holes in the walls. It hurt my fist to do so, but
at the same time it felt so good to release all that pent-up rage.

Repressed anger may be turned outward, and when it is,
often it's directed at the very people you love. It may show up
as blatant verbal or physical attacks, or be acted out in passive-
aggressive ways. Passive-aggressive behavior is acting like you
aren't angry when you really are and expressing it in indirect
ways. Forgetting to pick up the dry cleaning after you've promised several times you would, sleeping on your side of the bed
and pretending nothing's wrong, teasing unmercifully, and ig-
noring someone are all examples of passive-aggressive behavior.
Typically these are ways that you can express your anger without in fact appearing to be angry. You've learned them as a way
of sidestepping your anger, usually because you haven't learned
how to deal directly with anger without its being harmful or
destructive.

Another way for a man to deal with his anger is to turn it
inward and rage at himself. Self-destructive thoughts and behavior are a way for us to express what we were not allowed to
while growing up, and to do so in a way that doesn't hurt
others. Unfortunately, with this habitual way of dealing with

anger, we end up hurting ourselves. When you turn your anger inward, it can result in depression. Inner-directed anger is a strong component in depression, along with emotional numbness. If you have ever been depressed, you can probably remember the string of self-deprecating thoughts that typically accompany a sour mood, thoughts that can absolutely devastate your already fragile self-esteem. These thoughts are an explosion turned inward on the self, a way to beat yourself up with thoughts. Taken to the extreme and acted out, the end result is suicide. Once you recognize that these thoughts are your rage turned inward, the next step is then to externalize and express this anger in ways that won't destroy you—or someone else.

WHAT TO REMEMBER ABOUT ANGER

Anger is a feeling. As I noted previously, there is a difference between feelings and actions. As a man, you have learned to emphasize action over feelings. In order to deal more effectively with your anger, you must separate the emotion of anger from the notion that you have to act if out in any way, on others or on yourself. Although I will give you some ideas on how to focus and discharge your anger, there really is no need to *do* anything when you are angry, other than feel it. It may take something as simple as stating, "I am angry," to take some of the excess charge off.

Feeling angry doesn't mean you are right. This one is difficult, because we so love to be right. Still, adamantly believing that, no matter what, you are right, can lead to even greater hostilities, destructiveness, and violence. Wars are started because of at least two people thinking they are right and the other fellow is wrong. When you feel angry with someone, remind yourself that not only is your anger simply a feeling, but you also don't have to remain righteously positioned with your anger.

Feeling angry doesn't mean the other person has to change. We have learned so many ways to use anger to manipulate and control. If I growl at you, then perhaps you will feel bad and stop asking me questions. If I get angry and withdraw from you then you will likely feel bad for refusing to have sex with me.

Perhaps I will get angry and pout for several days to manipulate you into feeling bad about your having been upset with me. By using anger to manipulate and control not only are you alienating others, but you are acting out the adult version of a spoiled brat. If this is a problem for you, keep in mind that while you can certainly express your anger cleanly to another person, to try to use this very energized emotion for control is a bastardization of genuine feeling.

Anger and rage are not the same. They are certainly related, however. Anger, when it is cleared of all manipulation and righteousness, is actually quite stimulating and can often provoke and inspire action. When you are angry, the message that you're communicating can be delivered quite forcefully. Anger can help you set clear boundaries. There are other times when it feels good to let go in a burst of anger, not directed toward someone, but as a release of your frustration. Anger can motivate to action.

Rage, on the other hand, is primal. When you spontaneously and unconsciously regress to an earlier time of raw emotional energy, this is rage. It is the unmet anguished cry of a child in need, explosively delivered energy, unfocused and volatile, ready to leap in violent upheaval at the first available target. Rage causes damage. If acted out in an uncontrolled and unfocused manner, it can lead to violence and destruction. While it's not at all necessary to deny your rage, what is useful is to learn to tap into it and express it in a focused, cathartic way. A cathartic expression of this rage often reduces the sense of helplessness that frequently accompanies rage.

Behind most anger is a want. If you are angry with someone, ask yourself what is it you want from them. Quite often, you will find that you want them to act differently in some way, or you want them to give you something, or you want something else from them. For instance, if you're mad at your friend because he isn't listening, you want him to listen. The next step, then, is to ask for what you want. Keep in mind that you may not get it. If you don't, then you must decide whether to try to control your friend by staying angry, to tell him how you feel about his behavior, or to set boundaries if he continues with behavior that upsets you.

WHAT TO DO WITH YOUR ANGER

It doesn't work to vomit your anger all over somebody else. While this may unavoidably happen at times, it is a destructive expression of anger. If and when this does occur, what is likely driving the anger is some of the unresolved, unconscious rage from an earlier time in your life. If you find that your reaction is not in proportion to the circumstance over which you are angry, then this is probably the case. For instance, if you find yourself raging at your wife because she criticized the job you did in the garden, it's possible that you are overloading your present irritation with some unconscious anger/rage from past authority figures.

Another common way to mishandle anger is to keep it in hour after hour, day after day, only to find that a particular situation becomes a trigger for the release of this pent-up anger. If you are driving, for example, and somebody cuts you off and you then follow his car for miles trying to get even, looking for an opportunity to cut him off, then that other driver has become the scapegoat for a lot of anger and frustration that has been built up for some time.

Prevention is often the best medicine. Not that you should prevent yourself from ever feeling angry, because that would be an impossible task. Many spiritual and religious practices speak of "turning the other cheek" or of transcending, of rising above your anger. This is often just another justification for denying your anger. Instead, work with your anger consistently, preferably on a daily basis, so that you prevent a build-up of excess anger. By working with your anger you will also discover some of the triggers for this overlay of rage. Subsequently, when you do feel angry through the day, it will likely be much cleaner and clearer. The following exercises are all similar in that they provide a catharsis, or release, of your anger and rage, so that the tension doesn't have a chance to build up to the point of unconscious explosiveness.

Because, for most of us, anger is so frightening, these exercises may be hard to do at first. Go as far as you can, and be
sure to go just past the point where you're comfortable. Push
yourself a bit just outside your comfort zone, or if you are doing
these with a friend, have him push you. Whichever exercise
you choose, do it at *least* one time a day for the next two weeks.
Each time after you do, be sure and write in your journal whatever it is you notice, being particularly aware of what's going
on inside your body.

Exercise 9: Growling (A)

Find someplace where you can growl without disturbing anyone
else. This might be your bedroom or bathroom, your car, or
down at the beach when no one else is around. Open your
mouth as wide as you can comfortably, put your hand over your
diaphragm, and growl from your belly. Repeat this several times.
Growl as loud as you possibly can. The first couple of times you
try it, you may feel somewhat inhibited, but after that it will
probably get a little easier. It's important not to just do a throat
growl. You'll want to bring the energy up from your belly, your
gut, and expel it outwardly in sound. It's not a grunt, it's not a
scream, it's a full-bodied growl. So go for it and don't hold back.

I gave a married couple I was working with a variation of
this exercise. They were to growl at each other whenever one
felt some anger or irritation with the other. Nathan, the husband, reported back the next week that "It was really kind of
fun. Whenever Lisa and I were angry at each other this week,
we'd stop and look at each other eyeball to eyeball and just
growl. At first I was making a game of it, but then about the
third time I tried this I really could feel my anger. My gut was
tight, my jaw was clenched and so were my fists, and I realized
I really was angry with Lisa. I growled loud enough that the
neighbors could probably hear, but I didn't care. Lisa growled
right back at me, too, which helped. Afterward my throat was

a bit sore from the growling, but it was really worth it. I really like this as a way of expressing anger. It keeps it pretty basic."

Exercise 10: Growling (B)

A variation of the above is to work with another man, such as a friend, your therapist, or someone from your men's group. Both of you will get on your knees facing one another, about three feet apart, sit up tall, and put your arms out. Interlace your fingers palm to palm with those of the person across from you. The only ground rule is that you do not actually hurt one another. Then both of you push against each other, palm to palm, and while doing so, look in each other's eyes and growl. Keep doing this for about three to five minutes. This may feel awkward and bring up some nervous laughter in both of you, but even if it does, keep on doing it. Soon you will feel some real anger and perhaps some real rage. After you stop, talk to each other about what your experience was.

I was doing this exercise with a good friend, David. He had been talking about his anger toward his adult son, James, who had essentially cut David out of his life. We got on our knees, laced our fingers together, and started pushing and growling. I took the role of James. At one point as we were growling at one another, David's face changed. It turned red, the veins in his neck bulged, and he looked very violent. He let out a huge, deep growl that surprised me and pushed even harder, driving me backward. It was obvious that at that moment all of the hurt and rage he had been feeling and storing up toward James was being released in this momentary explosion. We stopped the pushing and growling, both of us breathing rather heavily. He shook his head and confessed to being surprised at the intensity of his reaction, admitting that there was a lot of buried rage there. He commented on how his shoulders felt more relaxed, and that it was a relief to do what we did.

Exercise 11: Discharging Anger

Another excellent way to release your anger and rage is by getting yourself a couple of good-sized floor pillows. Find a place where you can set the pillows down in front of you, and stack them one on top of the other. Kneel down in front of them, make each of your hands into a fist, and bring them down sharply onto the pillows while at the same time opening your mouth and letting go of a growl. Repeat this several times. Really let that energy move.

A variation on this is to get one of those large plastic bats, the kind you can get to teach a younger child to play baseball. Use this to hit with in place of your fists. Either way it's important to release sound as you release your physical energy with your hitting. If need be, you can have the pillow represent some person in your life, present or past. It's far better to beat up a representation of that person than to actually dump your anger on him or her. Again, if you have never done this you may feel self-conscious or silly, but do it anyway. It really will help you discharge a lot of stored-up anger and rage.

Paul, one of my clients, obviously had a lot of stored-up rage. In his parents' home, he was never permitted to express anger although he was continually criticized by an emotionally abusive mother. His father wasn't there for any support.

Paul has periodically had to deal with very debilitating depressions, a reaction to the tremendous discomfort he felt in being with others. Although there was more than this to his therapy, a turning point came in a session where he did some anger work, feeling his anger toward his mother. He was very nervous and self-conscious at first, but with some encouragement he hit the pillows in front of him very tentatively three times in succession. I prompted him to continue, and to feel whatever was there.

He started hitting again with his fists, and it didn't take long before he was truly feeling and discharging his rage. "I

HATE YOU! YOU NEVER LET UP! YOU WOULD AL-
WAYS PICK, PICK, PICK! AND YOU NEVER LET DAD
ALONE FOR ONE MINUTE! I HATE YOU!" Paul went on
like this for a few minutes, expressing a lot of the feelings that
he had never been allowed to get out.

Once this was acknowledged and released, much of his anx-
iousness and self-loathing was reduced. Paul began to understand that feelings often exist in parallel—love/hate, anger/hurt,
fear/rage. Discharging anger in this way wasn't a solution—but
it was a start.

"AFRAID? WHO, ME?"

Fear is another very fundamental emotion. It's the emotion in
us that alerts us to danger, that signals our bodies to prepare for
fight or flight. Unfortunately, we reach manhood conditioned
to fear certain things that are not life threatening, yet we treat
them as if they are. For instance, you may find yourself fearing
someone else's disapproval and treating this person as if the loss
of his approval would be life threatening. Or if you hold on to
the rigid image of being strong and silent, you may see behavior
that is anything less as a threat to your survival, when in fact
it may not be. Because we have so many habits like these, some
of our reactions and feelings of fear do not indicate some vital
danger; in fact we may need to challenge and confront them.

While it can still be useful to acknowledge the feeling of
fear, it is *not* always best to act on it. For instance, if you see a
fire and need to put it out, you must act in spite of your fear.
If you were on the battlefield with bullets flying all around you,
it would be literally life threatening if you expressed and acted
on your fearful feelings. Sometimes it is better to push the fight
button rather than the flight button.

Acknowledging your fear and acting on it in a situation
where there is some very real danger may be the wisest thing.
If you are about to walk down a dark city street late at night
and you feel afraid, your fear may be telling you something that

could save your life. There are a number of situations, however, where fear is merely a habit. In such situations, by acknowledging your fear openly and vulnerably, you will contradict your robotic conditioning that says you are in danger if you do so. Acknowledging your fear can open up communication between you and another person and enrich your relationships.

My daughters and I were in Vancouver recently to do an intensive five-day program of counseling. After some initial individual sessions with each of us, the counselors felt it would be useful to do at least one session all together. While I totally agreed, I realized that I had a tremendous fear of crying openly in front of my children. While I had done so once or twice before, I still had a tremendous fear of their seeing me sobbing deeply. I usually reserved that kind of crying for when I was in solitude. In large part it was purely conditioning, maintained by the fear that if I flat out cried I would somehow lose my authority as a father, they would not respect me, and they wouldn't love me anymore. While these were all certainly risks, they were minimal.

Well, sure enough, it happened. On about the third day we had our family session. Much of the grief about the divorce came to light for all of us as well as very strong feelings about a particularly nasty fight that had taken place between their mother and me about one year earlier. The counselor worked with Catherine, my younger daughter, in helping her to express directly to me some of her pain and anger about that fight. Catherine sat directly in front of me, hitting a pillow while saying to me, "I DON'T LIKE IT WHEN YOU AND MOM FIGHT." It was very painful, yet necessary, for her to acknowledge these feelings and for me to hear them. Yet, hear her I did. My face squirreled up and I started crying, blatantly and boldly. Once she had released a considerable amount of her anger, her tears came quite naturally, too. She didn't even look surprised at my emotion. I was agonized while at the same time delighted that this was finally coming out so directly. As I looked at her across from me, I spoke through my sobs and confessed to her. "I don't . . . like it . . . either. I know . . . it hurts you . . . when that happens." In spite of my fears, opening up and being vulnerable with my children has thoroughly enriched my relationship with them.

Exercise 12: Fear Inventory

The point of this simple exercise is for you to give yourself permission to have your fears, and to let others in on the fact that you feel afraid. In your journal, write at the top of one page, "I feel afraid of. . . ." Down the side of that page list all the things that complete this sentence. List not only things, but situations and activities. Write everything and anything down that comes to mind. As you do so, notice where in your body you feel your fear. As you pinpoint where in your body you experience the fear, make a note of it. Then share your list with another man. As you do so, see if you can touch into any of the actual feelings, again paying particular attention to what is going on in your body as you talk about these fears.

Linden shared his list with his entire men's group. "Well, frankly, at first I thought it was a stupid exercise, but I decided to give it a go. After all, what was it Roosevelt said? 'The only thing we have to fear is fear itself.' So I told them I wanted to try this, and they were very supportive. I started reading my list—'I feel afraid of heights, I feel afraid of losing my job, I feel afraid of snakes.' They all listened pretty closely. I was nervous, and my hands were shaking throughout, but I continued. 'I'm afraid when I share my feelings with all of you.'

"I paused, looked up, and noticed that Mark was on the verge of tears. I asked him what was going on—I knew I could get back to my list later. He came out with how he was afraid of losing his daughter in a custody suit with his ex-wife. This took us all by surprise since we were used to Mark being quiet, so we all focused on him for a while. From this point on, nearly everyone in the group opened up a lot more than they had previously. I eventually got back to my list, but now it was considerably easier to talk about my own fears. It actually felt pretty good to talk about them and be heard."

LOVE IS A FOUR-LETTER WORD

There's a great deal that can be said about love—including a slightly veiled implication that it is an obscenity. However, I want to focus on loving expressions that aren't confined to one specific type of relationship, such as a romantic one or the one you have with your children. As difficult as it might be to deal with any of the feelings we've focused on so far, for some of you this might be the toughest. To express love openly flies in the face of any "tough guy" image you hold about yourself. Though it's a paradox, you can be both tough and tender as a man. Yet as men we are handed a set of rules that limits how we can express our love and affection. To follow these rules, we either have to deny any and all expressions of affection or else make them very mild and constricted.

In healing your woundedness, you may find it extremely useful to push through your conditioned fear and take some risks in expressing your affection for others. This can take on many forms, but here we will focus on one: appreciation.

You can express appreciation in a number of ways, both verbally and nonverbally. The most direct way is to tell the person receiving your appreciation just what it is you appreciate. Statements starting with, "I like . . ." or "I appreciate . . ." or "I think . . ." or "I feel . . ." are the simplest and work the best. Be specific about what it is you appreciate. Rather than saying, "I really think you're a great person," find something in particular you like, such as "I really like how you listen so closely when we're talking." Say it directly to the person, rather than via a note or through a third party. Look him right in the eyes when you say it.

Exercise 13: Appreciating Others

Make a goal of offering at least two appreciative comments each day for the next two weeks. Each day make a note in your journal how it felt to express your love and caring in these ways. Be willing to take some chances. You can comment on people's actions, their looks, or their personality. Do not disqualify your comment by making light of it, demeaning it, or acting as if you don't really mean it. Make eye contact with the person receiving, and pause after you've made your statement for a reaction.

Gene wrote this in his journal: "Today I was with my good friend, Kirk. We were working on my deck, replacing a few of the boards. Afterward we sat out back and had a beer, and I got to thinking about how much his friendship means to me. I told him I appreciated how helpful he was and that I was glad he was a friend. We both made kind of a joke about it, something like, I always did have poor judgment. I didn't like that we joked that way, but I can see why we both did. It was new territory to say something like that."

Another step to take with love and appreciation is self-appreciation. As hard as it may be to love others, it may be even more difficult to love ourselves. Try the following exercise to gain a greater appreciation of yourself.

Exercise 14: Appreciating Yourself

Note in your journal as many things as possible that you appreciate about yourself. Include not only things that you do, but ways that you are. Come up with at least fifteen to twenty different items. Then, take the list and share it with a friend, preferably one who is doing the same exercise. Note your bodily sensations and your emotions as you do.

Curtis commented on this exercise: "It wasn't too bad writing the things out that I appreciate about myself. I came up with a few, and they're things I like to see in other people, too. Things like my friendliness, strength, and that I'm reliable. It was when I went to tell them to someone that it was hard. I didn't want to come off like I was bragging or being conceited. So I tried it with a good buddy, telling him it was just an exercise. I got through it, but he did tease me some. I just kind of rolled with it, and all in all, it felt pretty good just to say some of these things out loud."

5

Man to Man:
Friendships with Other Men

(Dean and Gordon are friends, having known each other for about two years. They are getting together for lunch to plan a fishing trip they soon will be taking.)

DEAN: How are you doing?

(I hope he doesn't ask me about what's going on with Kate. That fight she and I had this morning was a doozy.)

GORDON: Oh, I'm fine. A little under the weather this morning, but I'm feeling okay now. How are you?

(I feel lousy. My stomach is doing flip-flops. I'm not even sure I can eat anything for lunch. I'll just have to handle it.)

DEAN: Doing all right. I'm ready for this fishing trip. Are you?

(I'm nervous about this trip. I don't know Gordon that well, and I've never been fishing with him before. In fact, I haven't been fishing in years. I hope he doesn't like to talk a lot on these kinds of trips. I'm hoping to have some quiet time.)

GORDON: I can't wait. It seems like it's been a long time since I've been fishing. In fact, I think my last trip was about five years ago, with Vern, an old friend of mine who moved out of state.

(I wish I was going with Vern. I like Dean, but I don't know him that well. He says he hasn't been fishing all that much before. I hope he can carry his own weight.)

DEAN: I remember you talking about Vern before. He sounds like he was—or is—quite a fellow.

(Seems like he brings up this guy a lot. I wonder if he really wants to go fishing with me, or he'd rather go with him.)

GORDON: He is. I don't have much contact with him anymore. Just a phone call every few months. He moved to North Carolina. I miss him, but that's life. Say, how's Kate?

(It hurts to think of Vern and the fact that he's living across the country. I really miss him. He was one of my best friends. This is getting uncomfortable. I think I'll get the attention off me and onto Dean.)

DEAN: She's okay, but she's been under a lot of pressure lately. We had a few words this morning about my going away on this trip. You know how women are. No big deal. She'll get over it.

(Damn! He asked. I don't know how women are. I feel bad about the fight this morning. I really don't feel good about going if Kate's going to be upset. I felt like I should just call the whole thing off, but then I'd be pissed. Sometimes you just can't win.)

GORDON: Well, sometimes you're damned if you do and damned if you don't.

(It must have been one hell of a fight.)

DEAN: That's the truth. Anyway, let's talk about the trip. I want to get everything set before Friday.

(I'm glad he understands. I think it will be fun to go fishing with Gordon.)

GORDON: Sounds like a plan.

(Maybe it will be fun to fish with him. Dean's all right. I like him.)

Dean and Gordon went on to plan and execute a successful fishing trip, thus taking another step in their growing friendship. It's commendable that these two are even making the effort to be friends. Many men don't do that much. In many instances, once we are entrenched with our families and careers, our friendships with other men taper off or are simply nonexistent. We "go it alone," isolating ourselves from any close relationships with other males.

The way that Dean and Gordon are furthering their friendship is through an activity. Doing something physically active together is one practical way men can get to know each other. The above dialogue is focused around an upcoming fishing trip, yet other topics are brought up. We tend to be more comfortable in relating through our doing rather than our being, and this is why an activity can be a way to get to know one another better. Another thing you will notice in the dialogue is that there are a lot of unspoken feelings, sometimes even concealed behind pat phrases. This reflects how most of us have difficulty directly communicating feelings, especially to a man friend.

Through a commitment to developing friendships with other men, you can open up an array of possibilities that you otherwise would not have. Having male friends broadens your options. With a friend you can share activities that you might not ordinarily do, try new ones that you might not ordinarily try, and take up recreations that you had long ago given up. You may have played tennis when you were in high school, but gave it up for lack of someone to play with. With other friends, you would now have that option. Rather than confining your relationships solely to your wife and children—or if you are single, to women—with a man friend you again expand your choices. For instance, if your wife isn't available or isn't interested in backpacking, you can call up a man friend.

More specifically to having male friends, one major advantage to sharing your feelings with another man is that you can feel validated. Only another man can really know what it feels like to be a man. By mutual self-disclosure you discover ways in which your feelings are similar to other men's. While a woman friend may have some compassionate understanding of what it may be like to be a man, she is a woman. While a woman friend can certainly bring worthwhile elements to a relationship, they aren't the same as what a man can bring to a friendship.

Another benefit of male friendship is to fulfill a need that was frustrated when you were younger. That need was the need for fathering, which you had no way of getting from a father who was remote or altogether absent. Although you will never replace the missing father, other men now can give you the kind of male energy and attention that you never got from your father when you were a boy. There is a "mutual fathering" that goes on between men that is sometimes tough and incisive, sometimes quite sweet and tender, an exchange that can deeply satisfy this unmet yearning for genuine male energy and companionship.

Here we'll take a closer look at how certain cultural pressures have supported this isolation that has plagued most of us, and how these values, when upheld, can interfere with friendships with other men. From there I'll give you some suggestions on how you can develop and deepen your male friendships.

FROM ISOLATION TO FELLOWSHIP

I feel fortunate that there are now some men in my life I can trust wholeheartedly and that I consider to be part of my innermost circle of friends. I'm looking at a photograph of myself with some of my friends from the men's group I have been a part of since we started over five years ago. We had just come back from a rope course, where through some challenging physical activities we had put ourselves to a test as a group, as friends, and as individuals. I must say we all came through with flying colors. What I'm struck by in this picture is how much warmth, caring, and vitality show in our faces and our bodies. Much more than the physical challenges, the way we had supported and opened up to one another paved the way for even greater closeness and respect between us.

As I look at each man's face, I feel grateful and proud to call him my friend. We have been through a lot together, both in and out of the group. In Keith's face I see a wisdom that belies his twenty-eight years and a joy of living that is quite infectious. Thomas's face shows a newfound courage that came from confronting and overcoming his belief that he could not do these sorts of physical things. Ron's face has a steady glow and an engaging smile. His is a face you can trust, and the man matches what he presents. I admire each and every one for the unique qualities that he brings to the table.

Looking at this photo, I get both feelings of joy and sorrow. The joy comes because I am so glad to have these men in my life. I can truly call them friends and know that there is richness and texture to these friendships unlike anything I had ever known. And that's precisely what makes me sad. I simultaneously grieve over the fact that until the last few years I had not known friendships that could be so profoundly satisfying and rewarding. In all the changes that I've gone through in the last few years, one that I feel very thankful for is to have developed a few male friends whom I love and who I know love me. I think that this has been, and continues to be, critical to my own healing. In order to heal your wounds as a man, it is absolutely essential that you develop male friendships.

The Journey Begins

The notion of friendships with other men brings up a number of mixed feelings. I have memories of some really great times that make me smile, and some painful memories that make me feel angry and sad. The recollection of my days playing sports brings up feelings of pride and accomplishment. It was one of the only times as a young man that I felt a real sense of belonging and camaraderie with other men. We had a common purpose, a reason for being together. For men who have participated in team athletics, it's often true that this is the only time in their lives where they felt this kind of camaraderie.

Until these past few years I had felt extremely isolated for most of my adult life. My main source of solace and comfort, the primary way I met my need for intimacy, was by being in the arms of a woman. I didn't have a clue as to what a genuinely close, three-dimensional relationship with a man would really be like.

The men I called friends actually knew very little about me, which I'm sure is true for a lot of men. Being a "jock" throughout high school and college, my identity was completely intertwined with my athletics. As a result, I did most of the usual jock things—drinking, partying, and chasing women—but I always felt on the outside of the rest of the guys. There were things going on inside me that I knew I couldn't talk about with any of them. I enjoyed the fellowship and teamwork that came with being part of a sport, yet felt very timid when it came to making close friends with any of the other guys on the team.

As a result of my being so closed off and emotionally constricted, it was nearly impossible for me to get too close or too involved with anyone, let alone have a close friendship with a man. I was needless and unaffected, conveying the only image that I knew of as appropriate male behavior—that I didn't need anyone, and whatever life threw my way, I could handle it. Intimacy was too threatening because I had no idea how to be that close to someone. I was afraid that if I felt too close to a woman I would lose myself; if I felt too close to a man, that meant I was gay.

This is typical for American males. We are taught to value isolation, not to let anyone in too close, especially men. It's okay to have friends when you are a boy, a teenager, and into young adulthood, but once your career and your marriage are well under way, then male friendships tend to drop off. If you are like most men, by the time you are thirty years old, you may have work acquaintances, colleagues, or tennis partners, but no man you feel close to. You may be married and even feel your wife is your best friend and perhaps even have one or two other married couples you regularly go out with. Any male friends you do have are likely those you knew before you were married and with whom you probably have infrequent contact, such as a phone call once or twice a year.

What has been the norm is to be the "friendless American male," to maintain this isolation at the sacrifice of genuinely warm, caring, alive relationships with other men. Next we will explore first some of the causes behind our scarcity of close male friends, then look at some ideas on how to develop friendships with other men.

THE MALE MYSTIQUE

As noted previously, all the changes wrought in the last 150 years of the Industrial Revolution have had a major effect in all areas of a man's social and emotional makeup. This is clearly true when it comes to friendships with other men. In "A Time For Men To Pull Together," in *The Utne Reader* (May/June 1991), Andrew Kimbrell describes a distorted sense of values under which we operate that he calls the male mystique. He writes,

> This defective mythology of the modern age has created a "new man." The male mystique recasts what anthropologists have identified as the traditional male role throughout history—a man, whether hunter-gatherer or farmer, who is steeped in creative and sustaining relationships with his extended family and the earth household. In the place of this long-enduring, rooted masculine role, the male mystique has fostered a new image of men: autonomous, efficient, intensely self-interested, and disconnected from community and the earth.

When a man was taken out of the home by the requirements of the era, he became severely dissociated from his family and from the earth. The male mystique, the notion of a man as independent and powerful, became the new standard for manhood. This, coupled with a survival-of-the-fittest ethic, further emphasized a man's isolation, and stressed the importance of his success in the corporate world.

Kimbrell continues,

> The most tragic aspect of all this for us is that as the male mystique created the modern power elite, it destroyed male friendship and bonding. The male mystique teaches that the successful man is competitive, uncaring, unloving. It celebrates the ethic of isolation—it

turns men permanently against each other in the tooth-
and-claw world of making a living. As the Ivan Boesky–
type character in the movie *Wall Street* tells his young
apprentice, "If you need a friend, get a dog."

This "defective mythology" is what discourages closer ties
with other men. Culturally our ideal man is represented by the
isolated, independent, friendless loners, such as Dirty Harry or
Rambo. We've been raised with values that encourage us to
maintain distance between ourselves and other men.

KEEPING YOUR DISTANCE

That's been true for most of us: We have grown up with models
and values that preclude the kind of close, intimate friendships
with other men that, paradoxically, we are starved for. This
longing is masked behind cultural conditioning that has been
sustained for several generations, conditioning that dictates we
mustn't be too close or too friendly with other men. There are
three main barriers that interfere with deeper friendships with
other men: competitiveness, distrust, and fear of intimacy.

Competitiveness Above All

Not only does this keep us from our emotions, it interferes with
our friendships. In the male mystique model competitiveness
with other men is of prime value, overriding all other values.
This means: Watch out for yourself at all times, keep your eye
on the other guy, be wary and suspicious. You have to keep
your guard up with other men lest you be stepped on or pushed
aside. "Do unto your brother before he does unto you," becomes the rule for relationships with other men. This is most
evident in the cutthroat world of corporate politics.

In white-collar America, this competitive orientation further reinforces a man's alienation from other men. The pursuit
of materialism dominates. A man's worth is based on how much

money he makes, what kind of car he drives, the style of clothes he wears, rather than on the type of relationships he maintains with his family, friends, and community. A while ago I saw the ultimate statement of this orientation on a bumper sticker. It read, HE WHO DIES WITH THE MOST TOYS WINS. This attitude leaves me cold.

This relentless pursuit of bigger and better forces men to take a competitive stance with one another. It becomes necessary to hide all but those feelings and behaviors that get you the job or will keep you moving up in the company. There are usually several men, and these days women as well, competing for very few positions in the hierarchical corporate ladder. Troy sees this in the company he works for: "It's really cutthroat. Whenever there's an opening for a new position, everybody's lining up. There's one guy who I can tell has his eye on my job. He's always asking me lots of questions, acting as if he's eager to learn, but I can tell he's sort of checking things out. He won't get my job soon, but I'm sure he'll get some kind of promotion before long. He's eager, ambitious, and at closing time is always the last one to leave."

In most companies, there is no room for personal feelings and needs, and only those individuals who show ambition, aggressiveness, and a willingness to put aside their own needs will be considered for the job or the promotion. If you are open and vulnerable in this circumstance, the other guy may use that information to skewer you. Revealing personal feelings means that this information may be used against you, and that you may not get that particular promotion or position.

A successful manager, Grant was describing how after he had resigned his position in one company, he was somewhat perplexed about what to say in interviews with prospective employers. "The truth is I don't want to get back on the treadmill again. I really do want to have more time with my family and more time for me. But if I were to say that during an interview, I'd be screwed. I can just hear the guy's thoughts: 'Well, he sounds good, but I don't know about somebody who wants more time with his family. He doesn't sound very dedicated to me.

Maybe he's burned out. I'm not so sure he'd really work hard for this company.' I mean, let's face it. They're going to want somebody who is totally committed to his work and is willing to put his whole life energy into it. I'm not sure I'm willing to do that anymore, but I'm just not sure how to present that to the guy on the other side of the desk."

It's not only in corporate American that this kind of competitiveness can interfere with friendships. There are subtle yet harmful ways that we as men can put each other down, often unconsciously playing out a one-upmanship game of who has the most, the biggest, the prettiest, the fastest. Although sometimes this is harmless fun, there are times when this kind of exchange can hurt feelings, and hurt them badly, thus further alienating one man from another. Such competitiveness can be expressed subtly or by obviously putting down another man's accomplishments, feelings, or relationships.

I was very hurt by the reaction of my friend Brad, who is also a psychotherapist, when I told him that I was writing my manuscript for my first book, *Adult Children of Abusive Parents.* I was committed to completing it, yet felt the insecurities most new authors feel about their first book. I discovered just how much I looked to him for approval. I also became aware of how subtly competitive he was with the possibility of my success. The conversation went like this:

ME: It's a book for adults who were abused as children.

BRAD: Great. How have you researched it?

ME: Well, I've been reading a lot. Plus a lot of it is based on personal experience.

BRAD: How is it going to add to the present professional literature?

ME: What do you mean?

BRAD: You know, have you done any original research? Or is it going to add to the field so that other therapists can use it?

ME: Brad, it's not meant to be a book for professionals alone.

It's written so that anyone who identifies with having been traumatized as a child can use it in a practical way. I'm not trying to write the definitive work on abuse. It's a trade book, not a technical book, one that will hopefully be practical and helpful.

Brad's tone and demeanor carried a veiled criticism that the book would somehow not be "professional" enough or scholarly enough, even though that was clearly not my intent. I must say in Brad's defense that he was in the middle of his Ph.D. program, and I'm sure his orientation was toward his research and upcoming dissertation. Yet, this was an eye-opener for me. It showed me how this pattern of competitiveness had evolved between the two of us. Unknowingly, I had always been seeking his approval, but this was something I clearly had to do, with or without his approbation. We had another discussion where I shared with him my observations about our competitiveness, and my realization that I no longer looked to him for this kind of approval. Yet, in this initial experience, his unconscious competitiveness forcefully interfered with our friendship, even though it was only temporary.

Competitiveness is so ingrained and habitual that even when we are conscious of it, it may still jump out at us unwittingly. One time a friend and I decided to play a game of backgammon with different rules. The rules were as follows: 1) the goal of the game was for us both to win; 2) prior to each move we were to discuss it and mutually agree on the best overall move to achieve the goal; and 3) we agreed to pay close attention to what thoughts and feelings were going on within us throughout the game.

The game began, and there was a whole different sense through most of it. We both participated in the spirit of cooperation, spending time considering the various moves at different times during the game. I let him know what I thought the best move would be or he would let me know; we would then agree or disagree. If there was disagreement, we would state our opinions and discuss them until we ultimately found a move on which we agreed. All throughout the atmosphere was one of cooperation. About three-fourths of the way through the game, with it still being fairly even, I saw a move that he could make that would definitely put him at an advantage. I waited to see if he spotted the same move. We talked about the possibilities and it became apparent that he didn't see the move that I had spotted. I was calm and controlled on the outside, but gleeful on the inside, thinking, "Hah! I gotcha now!" I agreed with one of the moves he had chosen, knowing it wasn't the best overall move for our stated purpose. We finished the game, and although the white cleared the board before the black, we agreed that we had accomplished our objective. In our postgame wrapup, however, I confessed that for one of his moves I had advised the less effective move. In other words, because of this competitive streak, I had lied. Immediately following my confession, my friend disclosed that he had in fact done something very similar.

I'm not suggesting that all competitiveness is unhealthy or always interferes with friendships between men. If competitiveness is focused in games and is not taken seriously, not taken as a life-or-death struggle or with a "there are winners and there are losers" attitude, then it can provide a healthy release of instinctual, aggressive drives. Focusing competitiveness in these ways can sometimes help develop a friendship, especially as long as the focus on winning is not the priority and the competition isn't the dominant feature of the friendship. If it is, then you will both keep your guard up, which is antithetical to opening up the friendship. Strive for cooperation rather than competition.

Exercise 15: Non-Competitive Competition

Play a game with another man and follow the rules described on page 120 for the backgammon game. The simpler the game the better. It could be checkers, gin rummy, chess, or anything compatible with the purpose of the exercise. When you complete the game, take a few minutes to share with each other your observations and experiences. Ask yourselves the following questions:

1. What was the easiest thing to do in this exercise?
2. What was the hardest?
3. Did any old memories come up, especially ones of being competitive with other men?
4. Did you learn anything about yourself and your friend that you didn't know before you played this game?
5. How would you have felt if you'd done this with a woman?
6. How can you use what you learned from this in the rest of your life?

Walter wrote, "I played a game of checkers by these 'noncompetitive' rules with my eighteen-year-old son. I could see that this was as hard for him as it was for me. Maybe it's this father-son thing about competition. I kept thinking that he wasn't going to be honest about the way he played it, and I didn't trust him completely. I played by the rules, but I kept hearing this voice inside saying, 'I better win, I better win.' I didn't take it too seriously though. It was fun, and good for him and me to do this. It opened up another way of being together."

Distrust

A friend of mine, Jack, tells the story of how he was betrayed by another man. Over a period of several years Jack had been able to accumulate some savings, thinking that he would invest it someday. As Jack describes it, "This friend, Brendan—at least, I *thought* he was a friend—asked if he could borrow thirty thousand dollars for about six months. That was four years ago. He was going to invest it in this construction project that was just about completed. I figured that he was an okay guy. I've known him and his family for years, his wife and my wife have been in business together, our children played together. I never thought that he would screw me over, but he did. We made an agreement and signed it that he would repay the money plus a fair interest in six months. I have not seen the money to this day. When the payment came due I called him and called him and he never returned my calls. I finally went over to his house and confronted him. Almost got into a fight, too. He told me to my face that the money was lost and he couldn't get it back, something about the construction project went bankrupt. I was so mad—I still get angry when I think about it. I talked with an attorney who said because I didn't have anything to secure the loan, I couldn't do a thing about it. It makes me question my judgment about trusting other men now."

This is a second barrier to the close male friendships—our lack of trust in and for other men. Although each of us has his own version, like Jack, many of us have felt betrayed by another man, and perhaps have ourselves been the betrayers. If you are betrayed the natural reaction is distrust, and with a consistent experience of betrayal, the distrust builds up to become an impenetrable barrier to deeper friendships with other men. Distrust in other men can result from broken promises, violated confidences, or from being ripped off by another man. In these circumstances, the relationship is all but destroyed. After such an experience with another man, if you do maintain a relationship at all with him it will be even more superficial and distant. Jack has understandably severed all ties with Brendan, and with bitterness has all but given up hope that he will ever see his money again.

Your first man, father, may have set the tone for generally distrusting other men. Perhaps your father was abusive, alcoholic, or not there much of the time. Most men feel a vague sense of having been betrayed by their fathers as a result of his not being there in any substantial way. Some felt it very specifically, such as Robert, described in the second chapter, whose father, when he was a little boy, moved out of the way rather than catch him, saying, "That'll teach you not to trust anyone." Although the original source of your distrust is rooted in your relationships with your father and the rest of your original family, as an adult you may have had some experiences where you felt violated by another man that further reinforced your distrust.

One occasion that stands out for me happened with a man whose name is Russell, a friend I first met when I was married to Susan. He had just moved down from Northern California and was dating a mutual friend of ours. I was impressed with his perceptiveness and directness and took a liking to him. Russell had taken a big risk by moving and didn't have a job at first when he came here. So being the nice guy that I was, I agreed with Susan to let him move into our spare room, which we gave to him at no rent for about a month. I felt a bit awkward about it, but had an irrational need for him to like me. We actually did all right during that period and continued developing the friendship as time went on.

Shortly following my separation from Susan, I was feeling the need to affirm my friendships, particularly with other men. I arranged to have lunch with Russell, and from all appearances he looked and sounded as if I could count on him for support. We had an intense conversation over lunch, and I opened up considerably to him. I asked for his confidence in sharing something very personal and very private, and he agreed. I took a risk in trusting him, assuming from all experience so far that he was trustworthy. I let him know about the affairs I had had while I was still married, affairs I had never disclosed to Susan. I talked about my shame and my guilt over this and really opened my heart. There was some discussion over whether or not I should tell her about it. I was afraid to, and whether through avoidance or good sense, decided not to do so at that time. We parted after lunch and I had a good feeling about Russell, thinking that perhaps any reservations I might have held about our friendship were unfounded.

I found out I was wrong. About three weeks later in a heated exchange with Susan that took me by surprise, she informed me that she knew about the affairs. I admitted to it and she was understandably hurt and angry. In retrospect, perhaps it was the law of karma—what you put out you get back—but at the time

I not only felt a deep sense of shame over my behavior but tremendous hurt and anger over Russell's betrayal. Susan could only have gotten this information from him.

When I next saw Russell at a church we both attended, I confronted him.

"Did you tell Susan what I had shared with you in confidence?"

"No," he replied, looking me straight in the eyes.

"Well, she found out about what I had shared with you. How did she?" I pressed him.

"She asked questions and I gave a yes or a no," he answered.

"Well, Russell," I said, gritting my teeth, "that sucks. You broke an agreement, and I'm real angry!"

He didn't have much to say after that, nor did I. I have made a few attempts to reconcile the friendship since then, but he has given me no reason to develop any trust in him. It's a sad fact that this kind of violation undermines the very foundation of a relationship. It did between Susan and me. And it certainly did between Russell and me.

It isn't easy to rebuild trust once it has been broken, and if you've been hurt a lot by other men it will take time. This kind of violation is a deep wound. My rule of thumb in a relationship with a man is that it will take a minimum of three to four years to develop trust in him such that I can call him a tried-and-true friend. I like to be with a man through a variety of experiences, to see how he deals with conflict and adversity, how he plays, and how he deals with other people. Even then, I may get burned. As Gandhi was alleged to have said, "If you trust, you will be hurt; if you don't, you will never love."

Exercise 16: Trust Walk

This is a relatively simple exercise that will help you explore some of your apprehensions and considerations about trust, as well as help you focus on sensory experiences. You can do this one-to-one with another man, or if you're in a men's group you can do this by having everyone pair off and follow these instructions. Ideally, this should be done outdoors in a natural setting, such as a park with trees, a forest, or even a beach; however on one occasion in one of my groups we did this around the office building in which we usually met. Decide which of you will be partner A first—partner A leads, and partner B follows. Partner B wears a blindfold. Partner A leads partner B around by the hand, carefully guiding partner B's steps when needed. Partner A's job is to guide and take care of partner B during the trust walk, and to give partner B various sensory experiences by letting him touch, smell, feel, and if appropriate, taste different things on the walk. For instance, partner A could give partner B a flower to touch and smell, or ask him to stand still and feel the breeze.

It's important for partner A not to tell partner B the name of the objects he gives him, and for partner B to try to experience the qualities of the object rather than trying to guess what the object is. Talk to each other only as necessary for safety; most of the actual walk is best done in silence. After about ten minutes, switch roles. Once you have finished both ways, take a few minutes to discuss what you observed in both leading and following.

At some point shortly after this, write about your experience in your journal. For your discussion and writing, ask yourself the following questions:

1. Which role was more comfortable? More enjoyable?

2. As the follower, how did you feel trusting your partner?

3. If you were able to trust your partner, what thoughts and feelings did you have just before you found that you could do so?

4. If you had difficulty trusting, what thoughts and feelings got in your way?

5. Is this experience at all representative of your trust issues with others, especially with other men?

6. What was it like for you to lead someone who was dependent on you?

7. What was it like to be dependent on your partner?

8. What other feelings did you have toward your partner as either leader or follower?

9. Did this bring up any memories of other experiences where you either felt your trust betrayed or where you felt you betrayed another man's trust in you?

10. When you were blindfolded, how did you deal with the various sensory experiences?

Dana described what happened for him as part of a group that did this exercise: "Jesse and I did this one together. I chose him because I already felt like I can trust him. I led first—taking the lead was definitely more comfortable, and I actually liked it. I'm used to directing people anyway in my role as supervisor. I gave him some different things to touch—a leaf, a tree, a stone—and it was great watching his expressions as he explored these different things. When it came to my turn, I really got uncomfortable. I can tell because I joked and laughed a lot about it. I don't think I was ever totally comfortable throughout the exercise, even though Jesse did a great job. I did like doing the sensory stuff—it was how I imagine what blind people have to go through. Afterward, during our discussion with the group, I could see how most of my life I haven't been able to trust men. I'm sure it started with my father, because he would always tease me so much and play these stupid tricks on me, so I learned not to trust him. I think I have been basically trustworthy, but I'm not sure I've let myself get close enough to other men to ever have that tested."

Fear Of Intimacy

Several years ago I recall a comment my father made that typ-
ifies a man's reaction to intimacy with another man, particularly physical intimacy. We were at a family Thanksgiving
dinner, with the various subgroupings of kin. One group was in
watching a golf match on television, another was in the kitchen,
and a third was playing Nintendo. My dad and I had formed
our own subgroup out in the garage, and I was telling him about
how I was getting ready to make another move to a new resi-
dence. It was shortly after my separation, so my emotions were
close to the surface. At this point in our relationship we were
both somewhat used to occasional, very tentative hugs with
each other, although these hugs never lasted more than the
count of two, and both of us usually held our breath through
the approach, the actual hug, and the retreat. Afterward we
rarely made eye contact.

   At the conclusion of our conversation I was feeling quite
close with my dad, as was he with me. I stepped up to hug him
in a still rather tentative way. As I did so, I jokingly remarked,
"Well, if you didn't have that beard I'd give you a kiss on your
cheek." After retreating from the hug, my dad, hands in his
pockets, eyes looking out from under his eyebrows, said, "I'm
not one of those kind of boys." Clearly unstated was, "You
better not be one, either." I immediately felt embarrassed and
ashamed, as if I had done something very wrong. To ease our
mutual discomfort, we automatically laughed, and I muttered
something about, "Nah, no way." I felt even more uncomfortable because through my reaction I was somehow agreeing that
"being one of those kind of boys" was wrong.

   Like most men, you have probably learned to associate intimacy with sex, as in "I was intimate with her." You have also
typically sought to meet your needs for warmth, closeness, and
affection through sex and only through sex. Naturally with such
an equation your need for intimacy becomes bound up with
your sexual needs. To deviate from this formulation goes against
all that you have been taught to believe about what it is to be

a man. You dare not seek to meet your needs for closeness and intimacy from another man—it is simply too threatening.

There is considerable emotional and psychological risk for a heterosexual man to seek comfort and affection from another man. To do so stirs up some deeply ingrained fears that are often lumped under the term *homophobia*. Homophobia literally means the fear of the same sex, yet its common meaning is the fear of any sexual feelings toward the same sex. The sources of these fears are rooted in our culture and in the training we received as boys.

From an early age, boys are trained to "be tough," and not to cry when they are hurt. To do so meant you were a "girl" or a "sissy." It was okay to have a buddy, but you dared not be openly affectionate with him, or you risked similar derision. Girls could walk arm in arm, but if you did so you'd be labeled "fag." Your feelings of friendship could be expressed, but most physical touch was rough and tumble, just to be sure you wouldn't feel anything soft or tender for your best friend.

This fear is so reinforced that it becomes second nature. When men are together in tightly knit social groups, such as soldiers or policemen, group homophobia can become extreme to the point of actively persecuting gay men. By denying any sexual element to their being together, the group assures its sexual identity as heterosexual. The fear can then be projected as rage and anger against gays to further push away any implications in the group itself of any such proclivities. Thus demeaning jokes about gays become a way to express homophobia.

On an individual level, a man may even have unacknowledged and unconscious homosexual feelings. Because there is so much confusion between intimacy and sexual feelings, to have even a vague awareness of *any* homosexual feelings becomes extremely threatening. This doesn't mean you get an erection around men, but if you feel your love for someone, you are bound to feel some warmth in your body. This warmth can be confusing for most of us because we have so strongly associated it with specific sexual feelings, even though they may not be sexual at all. Even if you are gay, and have thus acted out these sexual feelings with men, you can have close, affectionate relationships without their being sexual.

For heterosexuals, aside from homophobia as an underpinning for fear of intimacy, our fears result from our childhood training. As a boy, if you were hurt you certainly did not seek comfort from father. If there was any comfort when you were hurt emotionally or physically, it more than likely came from mother. For most of us, it was rare that father ever provided comfort or nurturing. Father also became a model of how it was to be a man, and if your father was unaffectionate and subject to his own homophobia, as my father was, then you modeled yourself on this same sort of behavior. With the typical father relationships that we had, it wouldn't take too long to conclude that affection, nurturing, and intimacy among males are forbidden. And that's sad because, whether it's physical or not, we need intimate contact with other men. What you need to do to heal your woundedness is to develop closer, trusting friendships with other men.

Exercise 17: Intimacy with Other Men

In your journal, explore intimacy and the fear of intimacy with other men by responding to the following questions: Do you recall a time when you wanted to be close to another boy or man, but pushed him away, or got pushed away? Are you afraid of being called a sissy or a fag? Were you ever called this type of name? How did it feel? Have you ever called another boy or man a sissy, or questioned his being a "real man" in any other way? Why did you do it? How did it feel? Write about a man you have been intimate with. How did it feel? Did you ever back away from a friendship that was getting too close? Once you have written your responses to these items, share what you wrote with another man or with your men's group.

Jordan wrote a response to some of these questions: "For me, there's always been that fear of others thinking I'm gay underneath a lot of my friendships. In the past it's made it difficult to get too close to other men, and in a lot of ways has stopped my friendships from getting any deeper. And as much work as I've done on myself, it's still there to some degree.

"I live in a beach town that has a fairly sizeable gay population. The other day I was crossing the street and among the cars that had stopped there was a biker in full regalia—long hair, boots, the works—and I was looking right at him. He yelled out, loud enough for me to hear, 'You dumb faggot!' just as I got to the other side. It took a second to register that he had said that. When I realized it, I had a fantasy of flipping him off or yelling back at him—doing something to prove that I wasn't gay. Fortunately, I didn't actually do or say anything, because he looked like a pretty mean character. But that has continued to bother me since, so there's still some homophobic fears in here."

DEVELOPING FRIENDSHIPS

While there are certainly no formulas for developing friendships with other men, based on my personal experience and the experiences of others, there are some ideas that have been effective for myself and men I have known.

First, you must be clear that you want to have friendships with men. There is so much in the way of cross-generational conditioning that can interfere. In order to have men friends, you have to get past your anxiety about being close to other men by taking some risks toward making friends. The myth of self-sufficiency—that you are needless and unaffected—has to be set aside. As we've heard, "No man is an island," despite the fact that most of us have tried to treat ourselves as if we were. Remind yourself continuously that wanting men friends isn't wimpy or effeminate, it's one of the most natural desires there is, and is absolutely necessary to your healing.

As Gilbert put it, "Just about a year ago I realized that I had everything a man could want. I had a wife, a child, a home, and a job I enjoyed. It all looked perfect, and I felt like I didn't need anything else. But something was missing. One day while I was talking to another guy at work, it hit me. I didn't have any friends. Men friends. I was out of contact with the ones I'd had. So I made it a priority to have some men in my life that I could count on and be close to."

It's vital to realize that developing and maintaining friendships will take some time and effort. It will require you to make some compromises regarding how to spend your time. And time, these days, seems like such a precious commodity. If you are casual about your priorities, then you will have casual acquaintances. If having friends is one of your priorities, then you will need to invest some time not only in developing your friendships, but also in maintaining them. It will take a sincere commitment on your part to develop as well as maintain your male friendships.

If you are developing friendships, move slowly but steadily. True friendships do not happen overnight, so be patient and persistent in your efforts. Be willing to start conversations with men that you know or have met. These can be about the activity or setting you're in. Be willing to be superficial in your initial contacts. The conversation can move to more involved levels once you have gotten acquainted. With someone who is new to you, you will eventually know whether or not you want to get closer. If you find you have a good feeling with a particular fellow and some things in common with him, invite him to have coffee or a beer with you. When you are together, ask questions that help you get to know him but are not invasive or too personal. Tell him something about yourself that helps him get to know you.

Another effective option is to get involved with a prospective friend in an activity or a project, preferably one that is not directly tied in with work. If he talks about refinishing his deck at home, you might offer to help him with it. Perhaps you can help him with a speech that he is writing. Or maybe he is moving some furniture, and you could offer to help him move it. A structured activity gives you time together in a way where there are no obligations or expectations beyond the task at hand, yet it is an excellent method for interaction. I got to know my friend Bill better when he helped me build some bunk beds for my children. During the course of making them we each got to see how the other operated in those kinds of circumstances; we learned a lot about each other through conversations and interactions that were a natural part of our project.

Nurturing Your Friendships With Men

Assuming you have established an opening with a potential friend, or you already have a friend with whom you would like to develop a closer relationship, it's important to nurture that friendship. Be proactive rather than reactive. Instead of waiting for him to take the necessary steps, be the one to do so, especially in the earliest phases of the relationship. It may not seem fair that initially you will have to do most of the calling and arranging, but unless you already have an established relationship of some sort, that's usually what it will take the first several times. If at all possible, make plans to get together with him once every few weeks.

Once you have established a foundation of friendship, it helps if you sustain these efforts throughout the life of the relationship. Call with specific plans in mind. Other times call simply to check in and see how he is doing. One of my closest friends, Carl, has really taught me about this. I expect that if I didn't make any effort at all to contact Carl, I would still hear from him at least every couple of weeks. When I've been lax in my efforts to connect with him, he diligently calls me to see how I'm doing and report to me on his latest adventures with his wife or with his business. He has never once complained to me that he is the one always taking the initiative, nor does he ever seem to call out of a sense of duty or obligation. He is committed to our friendship.

As Carl said to me one time, "You know, Steven, most

people don't make the effort to maintain a friendship. But that's what it takes. It takes a commitment to maintain it. I make it a practice to call my friends regularly to check in and see how they're doing." Carl seems pleased just to talk with me, and it inevitably feels good to hear from him. From his example, I have learned to call him regularly, even if only to say hello.

We're at a time in the healing of our woundedness as men that requires new and more meaningful ways to "do" friendships. Rather than emphasizing competition and one-upmanship, we need to emphasize different qualities, such as cooperation and caring. Yet because of the powerful conditioning to which we are subject, to work these characteristics into your daily life, and especially your friendships with other men, will take consistent effort on your part. You will be going against the grain of how you were taught to be as a man among men and showing a willingness to go a little further than you may typically be comfortable with in your relationships.

That's why I call this section "nurturing" friendships, because that's exactly what it's going to take—nurturing. The root word for *nurture* is *nourish*. That's the kind of friendship I personally want in my life. We have more than likely had a limited experience of these kinds of relationships with other men, so we are all pioneers in learning to be better friends with one another. Rather than making log cabins in distant forests, this time the pioneering is on the inner plane, focusing on fresh and creative ways to be together as men.

There are certain characteristics that I have come to value in myself as a friend and in my friends. Conversations with others have helped refine these characteristics down to a few salient ones that are critical to an alive, growing, deepening friendship. While other qualities are certainly important, the most critical ones seem to be availability, integrity, vulnerability, and affection.

AVAILABILITY

At the risk of stating the obvious, you can't develop or maintain any close friendships if you don't make room for them.

Making room for friendships means first allowing the *time* for them. If you constantly don't have time, then you will never develop the kind of friendships you want. To do so you must put this on your list of priorities and then act on it. If you are constantly working seventy-plus hours a week, with the remaining time dedicated to your family, you won't have any time to be with friends.

Unfortunately, in our culture, work is no longer something we do just to earn a living. We become so identified with work that we lose ourselves. Work becomes our reason for being, and it becomes so enmeshed with the rest of our lives that we find it hard to tease out the time we need for ourselves for other activities. It's as if most of us have become slaves to our work. Granted that it may even be enjoyable, it's still sad that it has come to dominate our very beings such that we lose sight of other important things in life.

Sam Keen, in *Fire in the Belly*, has this to say:

> Something very strange has happened to work and leisure in the last generation. The great promise of emerging technology was that it would finally set men free from slavery and we could flower. As late as the 1960s philosophers, such as Herbert Marcuse, sociologists, and futurists were predicting a coming leisure revolution. We were just around the corner from a twenty-hour work week. Soon we would be preoccupied by arts, games, and erotic dalliance on leisurely afternoons. At worst we would have to learn to cope with "pleasure anxiety" and the threat of leisure.

> Exactly the opposite happened. Work is swallowing leisure. The fast lane has become a way of life for young professionals who are giving their all to career. In the 1990s Americans may come more and more to resemble the Japanese—workaholics all, living to work rather than working to live, finding their identity as members of corporate tribes.

This nearly religious devotion to work seems to be a way to encapsulate all of your needs, yet the high price of doing so is that the leisure time to spend strolling along the beach with a friend becomes consumed as well. The trap of not having time because of your work becomes a never-ending circle, where, when there is an opening, you fill it with more work so you can catch up or else get ahead! This combined with the hectic pace of the modern world makes it seemingly impossible ever to get off of the treadmill and pay attention to other things that are important in a man's life. Everywhere you turn you find more information to keep up with, more skills to acquire, and more tasks to accomplish. As difficult as it may be to shake out of this deadly routine, it's going to take a warrior's stand on your part to do so, to start by saying to yourself, "Enough!" and meaning it.

Although developing friendships with other men wasn't his only motivation, my friend, Jack, who I referred to earlier, decided to quit his job as a computer programmer and go into carpentry. "I was sick of it. I finished one job and the usual procedure was to hire out through an agency for another job. But this time I stopped and asked myself, 'Is this really what I want to be doing?' I guess my frustration had reached its limit. I wanted to be doing something I really loved. Yes, I made good money, but I was dying. I had high blood pressure, I was grumpy with my kids, my wife was always complaining about not doing things with her, and I had no time for me. It took awhile to line up some construction jobs, and during the interim a lot of people thought I must have been crazy. My income dropped dramatically for a while. Seems like I was always juggling bills, continually late with my house payments. It took about a year to fully get going in what I wanted to do. Although I worked hard, one of the side benefits of the change was that I had more time. Time for my family and time for my friends. I remember getting home early one afternoon and my wife and children were out. My usual routine would be to get busy with doing things around the house. Instead I called up a friend and invited him to go to dinner with me, which he did. We had a great time, and in fact since then have been getting together once a month."

Jack's method was only one of many for creating more time for friendships, and for you quitting your job may be too drastic a move. What it will take in order for you to be more available for friendships is for you to make a stand, to declare privately and publicly that this kind of availability is important to you. Making such a commitment opens the door for developing and maintaining your friendships.

Exercise 18: Time For Friendship

Sketch out how you spend your time. Of the 168 set hours in a week, you will most likely spend 56 hours sleeping, leaving you with 112 hours of awake time. By setting out approximate figures of how you spend your time, you can see how much time you actually have to dedicate to your friendships. This may seem like a very cut-and-dried way to go about it, yet doing so will give you very concrete representation of how you use your time, and show you more exactly how much time you have to devote to leisure and to your friendships. You may discover that you spend an inordinate amount of time with your work, or that you actually have gaps of time that are completely negotiable as to how you use them.

Now ask yourself exactly how much time each week you are willing to devote to developing and/or sustaining friendships with men. Write out an exact figure and consider this to be your goal amount of time to be available for friendships. Then make a firm commitment to follow through on this goal. From this, brainstorm possible ways that you can meet your goal actively by doing things with your friends.

Charles figured he has from two to five hours each week to devote to friendships. He found that although he thought he was extremely busy, by cutting out some of his television viewing, he could easily free up a few hours each week. Some of that time he decided to use playing with his two children. From there he allocated time with his friends. Every Sunday, if he hasn't already made plans, he calls one of his friends and sets up a lunch, tennis game, or some other activity for the following week. He has also joined an ongoing men's group. Through the year he may arrange some extended time with one or two of his friends, such as a weekend skiing trip. "It seemed a rather mechanical way to approach friendships at first, but I must admit it worked. I think writing it out like this helped me commit to the idea of being more available for time with friends. I've done this for a few months now, and I find I don't have to be quite so rigid with the scheduling part of it. Now I *know* just exactly how important my friends are and will never lose sight of that. If I don't spend time with my men friends, I find now I really miss it."

A trap in making yourself available is to do so with someone who is not. If you are trying to develop a friendship with someone who remains consistently unavailable, chalk it up to experience and look for someone who has more time for friends. There was a man in my Toastmasters group whom I really admired. We had lunch a couple of times and I found him pleasant to be with, yet he was usually unavailable. Although friendly and personable, he simply didn't have time for a friendship with me, being consistently busy with his work or his family. After taking the initiative several times I gave up. I got the distinct message that a friendship with him would be confined to Toastmasters meetings and very occasional lunches. Although I was disappointed, I realized that any friendship with this man would probably be limited.

Availability being the first characteristic that helps you develop and deepen friendships with other men, next we move on to another quality that adds an important dimension to any friendship: integrity.

INTEGRITY

In the dictionary the first meaning of *integrity* is "wholeness." We tend to view a man's integrity—his wholeness or completeness—as related to how honest and sincere he is. In other words, his ethics are on straight. Think of the men you know—or know of—whom you consider to have high integrity. Whether or not you agree with the men or their methods, you undoubtedly have a lot of respect for them as men. Gandhi, Martin Luther King, Harry S. Truman, Coach Kennedy (my high school coach), Spike Lee, and Kevin Costner are but a few examples of men that I personally admire for their integrity. These are some of the men that I can look to for inspiration. Even in the face of adversity, they have held fast to their principles. Not only do they talk their talk, they walk their walk.

Rather than trying to emulate an ideal role model such as these men or any others, what's important with regard to integrity in friendship is that you are trustworthy. You keep your agreements and treat your friends with dignity and respect.

The basis for trust in any relationship is quite simple: You do what you say you're going to do. If you make an agreement, you keep it. It's so simple, it's profound. For instance, when you say to a friend that you will call him, no matter how casually you say it, you have given your word. In doing so there is an implicit agreement. The automatic consequence of keeping your agreement, your word, is that it builds trust. The automatic consequence of giving your word and not keeping it is that it destroys trust. If you are casual or flippant about keeping your word, then you are likely to be casual about the friendship. When you give your word and don't keep it, another man may still be your friend but there will always be a wall built on broken promises between you and him. Making this a habit will prevent you from ever being more intimate with your friends. Plus it hurts when men don't keep their word.

There's one fellow I know that I like tremendously, but I don't trust him. He is charming, affable, and generous, but he has a habit of not doing what he says he's going to do. I would see him every once in a while, and he would tell me he was going to call me and then never would. Twice we made lunch appointments, and he canceled one and forgot the other, each time with great excuses. Whenever he would say he was going to do something, I completely doubted his sincerity and usually found that he didn't follow through. Recently in a telephone conversation I confronted him with my distrust. He was very hurt and angry, and defensive. It may mean that he won't be my friend anymore. I'll be disappointed, but my lack of trust in him was interfering with any closeness in our friendship.

Trust is such a delicate commodity, especially between men, that it is in your best interest to do nothing to damage that trust and to do everything you can to build it. For me to completely trust another man requires a few years. It take a variety of experiences with a man for me to know whether or not I can trust him. My closest men friends are those that I have known for a few years and have come to trust, precisely because they have passed all the tests with flying colors.

My friend Carl is a man I trust completely. He does what he says he is going to do, and has proven this again and again. In the earlier stages of our friendship, however, this was put to a severe test. He and I were working on an extensive writing project together, and he was coaching me in several aspects. I had come to rely on him for his advice and support and was feeling very good about how consistently he had come through. One day, after much complaining about how overworked he was, he started hinting at the fact that he needed to get away. I encouraged him to do so, reassuring him that I would be fine on my own for a few days. As that week went by he sounded more and more miserable, and I became more and more encouraging, telling him not to worry about me, that I would be okay. He finally told me he had arranged for a long weekend away for his girl friend and him, and I told him I was sure I could handle the project in his absence.

As the day for his departure approached, he seemed to need more reassurance than I did. Finally, the evening before his departure, he had come over to my place to do some work while I was out teaching a class. When I came home I found a note from him saying, "Bye-bye. Julie and I are headed off for the

Virgin Islands. We'll be back in ten days. Good luck. Love, Carl." I wasn't sure how to react at first. After all, he needed a break. He had told me he was going. The more I thought about it, the angrier I got. He had told me he was going for a few days. Maybe he had had this planned all along. I felt betrayed. Then I began wondering if there were other times when I had trusted him when I shouldn't have or that he had lied to me. I knew there was nothing I could do but wait until he got back, and in the meantime continue writing.

When he did get back several days later (although it hadn't been ten days), he called me. I first asked him how the trip had been. He told me he'd had a terrible time. The weather was bad, nothing had gone right at the hotel they had stayed in, the food was terrible, and he had felt bad the whole time for leaving me. I was secretly pleased that he'd had such a lousy time. I then told him I was angry, that I'd felt betrayed, and questioned my judgment about being able to trust him. He acknowledged he had been less than direct and honest about the trip, but truly didn't know where he was going or for how long until a few days beforehand. He then pointed out that throughout our friendship he has come through 99 percent of the time.

And Carl was right. During our friendship, this was the only time he had ever deceived me. It did take a short while for me to reestablish trust in him, and the record did support that I could do so. Today he is still one of my most trusted friends. There was a powerful lesson in that experience for both of us, and the conflict that we worked through deepened our friendship and taught us how vitally important integrity is in a friendship.

Another element of integrity is treating each of your friends with dignity and respect. This means not to try to "screw him over," to take advantage of him in any way, shape, or form. You don't lie, cheat, or steal from him. You don't do anything that is intentionally demeaning. You don't put him down when you're with others. You extend your care for this man in all that you do, and by so doing generate an even deeper quality of trustworthiness. Perhaps an ultimate test of how trustworthy you are is if your friend would leave his children and his wife in your care for several days while he went away. Could you pass the test?

Exercise 19: Men of Integrity

Think of men of integrity you admire and write out their names. Next, write down the specific qualities in these men that you find attractive. Do you see these qualities in yourself? If not, what can you do to develop these qualities? What are some other ways that you are trustworthy? In what ways are you not? Write the answers to these questions out in your journal. Talk about them with a man friend, or else bring them up for discussion in your group. If you do, I'm sure it will generate a lively discussion, because trust is the foundation for any strong relationship.

A shining example of integrity on my personal list is Mahatma Gandhi. He took a very specific stand for freedom, challenging the British Empire as a matter of principle. He did so nonviolently and was a deeply spiritual man. Another example is Martin Luther King. Who could ever forget his speech that began with that most stirring statement: "I have a dream." His courage and moral conviction were not only an inspiration for other black men and women, but for people of every race, creed, or color. He gave his life for what he believed in.

In another vein, one of the men I admire is Kevin Costner. I recall reading how he had made the movie *Dances with Wolves* in spite of everyone's warning him that it was too long, that you couldn't put dialogue translations on the screen, and some other objections as well. In spite of this, he did what he thought was right, and the rest, as they say, is history. *Dances with Wolves* went on to win the Academy Award for best picture.

I like Costner's tenacity, his willingness to go against the grain, to tell the truth as he sees it. I also read somewhere that he still hangs out with his friends of many years, even though he has achieved superstar status. Although I don't actually know him, everything I've read and seen I admire.

Then there are men who don't necessarily achieve public acclaim, yet are to be admired for their integrity. My friend Paul comes to mind. He has held his head up with dignity through considerable adversity over the last few years. I admire his tenacity, durability, and honesty. Another friend, Noah, is in the real estate business. He is successful at what he does precisely because he follows his ethics and principles. He is exceptional at following through, for doing what he says he is going to do, and for really trying to play fair. When you do the above exercise, think both of men who are known to the public and ones you know personally.

VULNERABILITY

Another characteristic that is an especially important ingredient of stronger and deeper friendships is vulnerability. This particular characteristic goes against everything you've been taught about what it takes to be a man, yet it's essential to healing your woundedness. Vulnerability seems like the antithesis of toughness, and sometimes it is. There are times when you need to forget about being vulnerable and be as tough as you can be. Being a soldier in the battlefield is an example of where being vulnerable would cost you your life. Yet in many other circumstances, especially in relationships, the ability to be more tenderhearted is what will open the door to true intimacy. What I most like about being a man is that we have the potential to be *both* vulnerable and tough, and to express the quality that is most suitable for the particular circumstance at hand.

Being vulnerable is not a call for men to be soft. Men who are soft and sensitive all the time are usually missing a certain dynamic vitality. You may not even notice them much. What is missing are the qualities of fierceness and resolve, the instinctual wildness portrayed by the "wild man" described by Robert Bly in *Iron John*. This balance of tender openheartedness and wild-man energy can lend itself to creative, expressive, three-dimensional relationships with other men.

One note: There are men you shouldn't open yourself up to for a number of reasons. You have a sense they will take advantage of you or demean you or else you have a history with them that says they tend to do so. Even though I still have a distant relationship with Sam, there is no way I will be vulnerable and open with him again. I have told him of my feelings of betrayal on other occasions, yet I still feel a deep distrust of him. On this call, I totally trust my own instincts.

One of the prime ingredients in being vulnerable with another person is *self-disclosure*. Self-disclosure is when you give the other person information about yourself. The information you give can be one of two broad types: factual or personal.

Factual information is the what, when, and where about you. Giving factual information goes beyond the superficial "How are you doing? I'm fine" that reveals nothing at all about you, yet falls short of revealing anything of a more personal nature. In our interactions with other men, this is often as far as we go. We tell other men about what we do for a living, specifics about our jobs, about our families, last year's vacation, or last weekend's football game, but little inside information. Or else we keep tightly closed and, if there's any interaction, we ask a lot of questions and listen to the answers, letting the exchange be one-sided and therefore relatively safe for us. I used to pride myself on my ability to keep the attention on the other person by asking a lot of questions without revealing much at all about myself. It kept me safe, but didn't get me any closer to people.

By at least sharing some factual information, you let your friend get to know something about you and thus open the door a bit. This type of disclosure may be perfectly appropriate at the beginning stages of a friendship. You may be testing your new friend to see what he's like. If his responses are typically demeaning or teasing, then you may not want to go much further in self-disclosure and being vulnerable. (On the other hand, you may want to tell the truth about how such behavior makes you feel.) Many of us are unwilling to test the waters much further than through disclosing factual information, and thus our relationships with other men stay rather impersonal and on the surface.

Peter commented: "I went to a party last night—it was a fairly large group—and had the opportunity to meet quite a few people. Two things I noticed about myself: First, I was a lot more comfortable meeting women than men. Second, when I did meet other men, usually the first or second question we would ask each other was 'What do you do?' It seemed like we couldn't get past our 'doings' to really get to know one another." And how sad it is that this has typically been true when meeting other men.

Exercise 20: Just the Facts

For the next two days observe how much of your self-disclosure with other men is factual and how much is personal. Observe how you communicate in different relationships. Factual information alone may be quite appropriate in certain relationships—such as the banker, or grocery clerk, or with someone you have just met. You're not going to communicate the same way in every relationship. Some relationships will remain distant, others more personal. However, begin to notice opportunities with friends to share more personal information, and observe what you reveal with these friends. Note whatever fears you may have of sharing more personal information. Write out your observations each day in your journal.

Gary described his experience with this exercise as being quite enlightening: "I see how much of the time I spend in talking about details, but not much about substance. I also see how quick I am to pull back if the man I'm with reacts at all to anything I say of a personal nature. I was with a guy named Tom, somebody I work with, talking about this and that. Somehow the conversation led into children, and I started telling him about how I felt when I watched my three-year-old daughter sleep. He gave me a look like he thought I was being kind of weird, so I quickly laughed it off and made a joke about it. It just showed me how scary it is to open myself up to someone."

To open up further to another man requires a different sort of courage than it takes to climb high mountains or jump out of airplanes and parachute to the earth. It takes the courage to lay down your armor and expose your belly, not to the enemy, but to your friend. Self-disclosure of this variety is to expose more personal information. This goes beyond the facts, into your *feelings* about those facts. Not only what you do for a living, but how you feel about it. Not only how many children, but your feelings about them. This next level of self-disclosure can move into even riskier yet exquisitely gratifying territory of what you are feeling *right now*, rather than about something peripheral to the moment. If you are feeling sad, you feel and express your sadness at that moment with that person. If you are scared, you let the other person know you are scared. If you are grieving, you let him in on your grief.

Exercise 21: Revealing Yourself

Once you have spent a couple of days observing your factual self-disclosure to other men, spend the next week taking some risks with more personal self-disclosure. To start, risk expressing milder feelings such as irritation and disappointment and then move on to more intense feelings like sadness, hurt, anger, and love. Take the risks with friends where there is a reasonable chance that your feelings will be received and won't be mocked. Record daily in your journal what your experience is.

A few years ago I went out to dinner with my friend Bill. While he was telling me about his plan to ask his girl friend, Sandy, to marry him, I had a lot of feelings about the idea, but at first was reluctant to share them. I thought, what if he doesn't like what I say? What if he stops being my friend? What if I'm wrong? So I took a deep breath and launched, starting with the seemingly innocuous question, "Do you want to know what I think?" I must say that whenever I've asked this of someone, I've never been refused. Bill said, "Sure." So I continued, "You know, Bill, I don't feel good about what you're saying. You've only been dating each other for a few months. I think it's much too soon. I think she's a wonderful woman and I hope you two do get married someday, but slow down. Live with her, date her, love her, but don't get married yet." I knew that once I said it, I could let it go and Bill would decide what he needed to do.

He didn't say much after that. The conversation switched to talk about camping and motorcycling. I had taken the risk and said what I needed to say about my feelings and my judgments concerning the situation. He decided not to get married, but I was distinctly aware that for several weeks afterward he was rather distant and cool. Later, in his own self-disclosure, he confessed to me that he had been pissed off at me. Yet in spite of his anger, he had heard what I had said, and it apparently struck a chord in him. To this day Bill and I continue to be the best of friends.

AFFECTION

There is a powerful and memorable scene in *Dances with Wolves* where Lt. John Dunbar, who was given the Lakota name Dances with Wolves, is preparing to leave the Lakota tribe that had become his family. He and his wife were leaving because his continued presence would endanger the tribe. One of his friends from the tribe, a fierce and fiery warrior named Wind in His Hair, is on his horse atop the ridge a few hundred feet above the trail Dances with Wolves is about to take. Wind in His Hair is shouting for all the world to hear, "Dances with Wolves, can you see that I am your friend? Dances with Wolves, can you see that I am your friend?"

This was such a potent expression of the affection that Wind in His Hair had for Dances with Wolves that it left me in tears. How willing am I to express affection to my men friends, whether it be through words, action, or touch? How much am I willing to come out from behind my facade and let my friends know how much I love and care for them? Although I find it is getting easier to show my affection for the men friends I have, I still come up against stumbling blocks in the form of my fears, which at times are only vaguely defined, and at other times are very clear. I fear showing my affection because of what my friend might think of me and because I simply have not been used to being openly affectionate with another man. I'm not used to letting another man know of my positive, endearing feelings for him. As discussed earlier, most of us have difficulties with feelings generally, let alone warmth and affection.

Affection can be shown in many ways and comes in many forms, but generally there are two. There is noncontact affection, such as admiring, complimenting, appreciating, and gift-giving; and there is contact affection, which is nonsexual hugging and touching. We may be accustomed to sharing affection in these ways with women, but for most of us, these are revolutionary in friendships with men. Showing affection in these ways is something I usually do with men I have known for a while or in workshops or gatherings where there is permission to open up and share affectionately. There are times when it's quite easy to do so, and other times where I tend to freeze up and/or withhold.

As to noncontact affection, in order to show this you must be willing to risk opening your heart. Instead of seeing your friend as an adversary or someone to be feared, see him as being on your side. Appreciation, which is a loving gratitude, is one form of expression we worked with in the previous chapter. Another similar expression of affection is admiration. Admiration tells the other person that you respect him, that you have the utmost regard for him.

You can offer your admiration in very specific terms, such as, "I really admire the way you are able to listen to others and pick up the subtleties in what they are saying," or "I really admire how you have stuck with this project in spite of the setbacks." Whatever it is, offer it openly and honestly. Robert Bly has made the particular point that younger men need the admiration of older men. We can broaden this to include men of any age admiring other men.

Admiration is but one form of affection; another non-contact form is to openly and blatantly express your love. After being in a group together with a few other friends, doing some emotional healing work, I got a call from Jack the next day. He said, "Steven, I called to tell you that I love you, and I think you're a neat friend." At first I almost dropped the phone because it was so unusual for Jack to be so open with his love. Tears came to my eyes, and I said nothing for a few seconds. I wanted immediately to say something, but that would have seemed to be a diversion from really letting what he said in. I thanked him, and told him I liked how we were getting to be closer friends, and that I totally admired him for taking the risk in calling me to tell me what he did.

Exercise 22: Admiring Other Men

For the next two weeks, look for opportunities to express your admiration to men that you care for. Do so with friends and with men you aren't necessarily that close to, but whom you do in fact admire. Remember to be specific and direct. Even if the other man has some discomfort with this, don't let that stop you. Keep your statements brief, but say enough to get your point across. Also, call or write men friends who have moved away but to whom you still feel connected. Call those men that you have been meaning to call but haven't gotten around to yet. As you practice expressing admiration in these different ways, write out your observations in your journal.

Justin made an effort to do so and was pleased with the results. "It felt good to do this. Inevitably the men I made comments to reacted very favorably—they liked it. There were times when we both ended up joking away the compliment. I think that's how we guys deal with feelings when they're uncomfortable. I told my friend Darrel how I really admired his way of always being there for me when I needed him, and his comment was, 'So, what's going on? You need some money or what?' We both laughed, but it occurred to me later that it was hard for both of us to deal with my comment."

Another option is gift-giving. A small, very meaningful gift that is given not out of obligation but out of thoughtfulness and affection is the kind of gift I like to give and like to receive. I remember one time when Phil gave me some tortoiseshell guitar picks. It meant a lot because he and I played guitar together frequently and he knew that I liked this kind of pick. I have another friend who every so often sends me a friendship or thank-you card. It's delightful receiving these cards, and this continues to expand our friendship and my love for him.

Exercise 23: Gift-Giving

Think of a man friend to whom you'd like to give a gift. Let it be something simple, such as the guitar picks that Phil gave me. It may be something that you find in nature, such as a rock or a seashell that is imbued with meaning. Think back on the kind of special gift you might have given a buddy when you were eleven or twelve. Then go ahead and find the gift and give it to him.

My friend Carl frequents stores that typically have very unusual items, many on sale. From time to time when he visits he will bring with him an item to give to me. Since these are often out-of-the-ordinary gifts, whenever I see them or use them, I always think of him. On the last visit he gave me a pickle snatcher, which is a device that when you press down on the top, extends four tiny wire arms with sharp ends that will then clamp together around whatever object (such as a pickle) is in place when you release the top plunger. As they say, it's the thought that counts! I think it's a great gift, mainly because it is one of the ways he expresses his affection for me, and whenever I see it or use it, I think of him.

Showing affection via contact may be a little touchier (pun totally intended!) because it can really raise all of your fears about being physically close with another man, including your homophobia. You don't have to start right away with outright hugs. Start with small gestures of physical affection such as a hand on the shoulder or upper arm. For instance, when you are talking with your friend and you say good-bye, if you shake hands, put your left hand on his right forearm. Let any of this kind of touch be natural and not forced. If and when you are ready to take the risk, you can hug. Start slowly. Perhaps the first time you hug a friend you will hug him shoulder to shoulder. From there, hug face to face. If this is new for you, expect to be somewhat uncomfortable, and expect your hugs to be short. Whatever your preference, let the hug be suitable for your particular comfort level.

Exercise 24: Touching

Experiment with different kinds of touch with your men friends. By paying close attention and taking some chances, you will likely encounter your fears (if you have any) of physical affection with another man. Also, be aware of any reactions on the part of others. Most men are not totally comfortable with physical affection, so be sensitive to this, but don't let negative reactions discourage you. Record your experiences in your journal.

I described earlier my father's reaction to one of my first attempts to hug him, the message clearly being that "real" men don't do that sort of thing. Yet now I find that with my closer men friends, if I don't get a hello and a good-bye hug, I feel like I'm missing something. (I do have a pet peeve about hugs, however. I do not like to be patted when I am being hugged. I find that a lot of men do this, probably to ease the discomfort and send a nonverbal message that says I'm not going to get too close.)

Now that we've looked at some ways to heal the woundedness between men and thereby deepen your friendships, let's move on to an area of friendship that has its own complications and its own rewards: relationships with women.

6

Women as Friends
and Lovers

My former wife and I sat in the waiting room, both making some nervous conversation about the children while awaiting Dr. Johnson's arrival. I was twitching inside from nervousness, doing my best not to show it. Susan and I had been divorced for over six years, yet still there were a lot of old wounds between us that had never completely healed. We'd had stretches of time when we'd gotten along fairly well, plus a few good arguments and one very painful fight that got physical. I had no illusions about us ever reconciling.

The main reason I had initiated this session—agreeing to go to her counselor—was to do whatever it took to clear up the old hurts so that our two daughters, Nicole and Catherine, would not continue to be dragged down into the garbage that went on between Susan and me. No matter how she or I tried to hide our pain and anger, to pretend that everything between us was fine when it wasn't, the girls would pick up on it.

Dr. Johnson arrived and we stepped into his office and got started. As the session progressed, it became apparent that there were a lot of feelings that each of us hadn't acknowledged. Emotions got more and more intense as we moved past simpler issues such as my buying the children some new clothes. Finally, as feelings came up about the past, we moved rather heatedly into some of the core issues.

ME: What I want to know is why you are still carrying around so much hurt and anger toward me. I mean, it's been over six years.

SUSAN: Why? Because you lied to me when we were married. You had your affairs. We even went to counseling and you never said anything. Was the whole marriage a lie? I can't believe that I didn't see it. It still hurts!

ME: Yeah, I lied to you. I know I hurt you, and I'm sorry. I didn't know how to be close, and I didn't know how to be married. How could I let you know me when I didn't even know me?

SUSAN: You could've tried. You could've said something. I trusted you. I really trusted you.

By this time we were both in tears. Dr. Johnson sat back, not saying much. He didn't have to. It was painful but necessary to hear and to feel the truth. I couldn't disappear into my shame or into counteraccusation anymore. I acknowledged that I had lied, that I had betrayed her trust and, by doing so, had hurt her very deeply. I was tired of beating up on myself for what I had done. The affairs were just another way to keep myself distant from her, not to let her know me. Through all this, what I realized I wanted from Susan was for her to see that I had changed, that I had learned something in the nearly seven years we had been separated. I wanted her to see me for who I was now, not who I was then.

SUSAN: Well, I think you do feel bad. You're different somehow, but I still don't trust you to be the way you say you are.

ME: That pisses me off! You don't have to trust me! You don't have to believe me! I don't expect you to. I just want you to see me for who I am now.

SUSAN: Well, I'm still not sure. And, no, I don't trust you. I don't trust that you are who you say you are.

ME: Susan, I have changed. And if you can't see that, I can't prove it to you. I don't expect you to believe me, or to all of a sudden trust me. I just want you to see me now.

SUSAN: Well, you hurt me and I—

ME: I know I did, but that was then. I want you to see me now! JUST SEE ME! SEE ME!

This emotionally charged encounter with my former wife summarizes the dilemma I've been in with women through most of my adult life. I confess that I still don't have women altogether figured out, nor am I always clear what relationships with women are all about. What I do know is that through a lot of painful experiences, grief over broken relationships, and a lot of trial and error, I'm beginning to make some sense of what was at one time completely mysterious: women, and how men relate with women. I am also clear that I will never completely know what it's like to be a woman. I can understand, relate to, find parallels with, but I will never *know* what it's like. But as I heal my woundedness and touch into a greater depth of my being, of my maleness, and as I find strength, closeness, and compassion with my men friends, I have seemed to more naturally understand, honor, and cherish the feminine. As I do so, I find that my relationships with women are more creative and diverse. I am also certain that, for any of us, understanding our relationships with women is an open-ended journey of discovery. For me it has been a process of letting go of a lot of old habits that have prevented me from ever being too close with a woman.

With any partner, including my former wife, I've been scared to show too much of myself for fear that I would somehow lose myself and lose my manhood. I've hidden a lot of my feelings and needs, trying to remain invisible, and if there was any threat that I might be seen I would find some way to run into the arms of another woman or behind the smoke screen of my cigarettes or the mellow dopiness of a joint. If none of those was available or wasn't working, I could always resort to acting dumb, pretending that I didn't know that I was hiding away. I could even turn the situation around so that her efforts at finding me and her frustration at not doing so were her problem, not mine.

Yet paradoxically, as I so vehemently was saying to Susan

in the session, I yearned to be seen—to be seen by a woman I cared for as the man I was, behind the macho wrappings, behind the sensitive male act, to the heart and guts of the self that was so much more than these posturings, yet included all of them. I ached to be held and comforted, simply to be loved by a woman without having to prove anything, without having to earn her love or feel obligated to give her something back. Sex had become the only thing through which I could come close at all to this.

I've played out some variations of this conflict in a few relationships, alternating between my need to be close and loved by a woman and my need to feel separate and apart from her in order to distinguish myself clearly as a man. I was never quite sure how to resolve this other than by quietly and covertly keeping my distance while at the same time avoiding any behavior that might earn me outright rejection. This was something I had learned to do for as long as I can remember, starting with my first relationship with a woman: my mother. In order to understand more fully our present-day patternings in relationship to women, that's where we must start.

THE LEGACY OF MOTHER

It's in this original relationship where you first learn about Woman, and it sets the precedent for your relationships with women in your adult life. Although there are other influences, particularly how your father acted with your mother—passive, abusive, submissive, loving—many of the conclusions and generalizations you have drawn about women are based on any love and nurturing as well as any wounds received from the first woman you ever knew.

In addition, how you dealt with the conflict between your need for a woman's attention and affection and your primal fear of being swallowed up by mother/Woman becomes a key to understanding your present-day relationships with women. You may reenact this conflict by avoiding intimacy altogether, by keeping the woman at arm's length but not too far away, or by being seductive and sexual but unavailable for a relationship. You may reenact it by trying to please women all the time to avoid their rejection or displeasure, or you may behave in a passive-aggressive manner, wherein you look and act as though you're trying to please while covertly rebelling against the female authority that you have projected onto your mate. Whatever your particular modus operandi, to understand more clearly how you developed that pattern, you have to appreciate the wounds you received from your mother.

Too Much Or Too Little

We've all be wounded in some way by our mothers. In fact, the initial wound of separating from mother is ultimately a necessary and healthy one for a man, his first step into manhood, but one most of us have not fully experienced.

Aside from this wound of separation there are other ways we can be hurt in this original relationship, ways that are not so healthy and that will distort how we later relate to women. Typically the deepest wounding comes from extremes, where we receive either too much or too little of mother. She was either *engulfing* or *abandoning*. Within these two styles of relating there were other types of injuries you may have gotten from your mother, but these two styles of relating provided the foundation for any other traumatic interaction.

ENGULFMENT

If your mother was engulfing, she more or less "swallowed you up." You felt at the least dominated, and at the most suffocated. She may have done this overtly and aggressively, or more subtly, by manipulating you with guilt. If your mother was engulfing—and this was the case for the majority of us—it was hard to see yourself as a separate person. In trying to mold and manipulate you by discouraging your independence, rather than encouraging and respecting your individuality as a boy and later as a man, she may have been acting out her own needs for intimacy with a male through you, especially if your father wasn't available and you were essentially a captive audience. You may have unwittingly taken on the role of "mom's little hero" in order to earn her love and in order to meet a lot of her needs.

This style most closely describes my relationship with my mother. Recruited to be her "little man," I was an unwitting ally in the unspoken conspiracy against my father, as well as a source of comfort for her when she was ailing physically or emotionally, which was often. I tended to her ailments and learned to be a really good listener.

When I was twelve years old, my other brothers and sister had all graduated from the home into lives of their own, and my father, mother, and I made the move from Iowa to California. My dad could not find work in his chosen trade for some time, so he ended up taking just about any job he could get to support the family. His drinking worsened, and my mother seemed very helpless, frustrated, and depressed much of the time.

At times I felt like both a mother and a husband to her. I felt a vague uneasiness with my father, a competitiveness that I couldn't at that time define. I secretly felt inside that I could treat her better than he did. Something felt wildly out of place with this, but I had no way to understand what it was.

Once, after my dad stormed out of the house, she burst into tears. I took charge, told her to sit down on the couch. I got her something to drink, and took the chair at the side of the couch and set it out in front of her so that when I sat in it I was facing her directly (it's no accident that this positioning is similar to how I sit when I'm counseling people today). We talked—or should I say, she talked while I listened—and I commiserated with her on what a bastard my dad was; she had a right, I agreed, to be hurt with the way he treated her. I felt right at home in my role with her. I had her wholehearted attention and appreciation such as I didn't have at other times, and I was quietly pleased that she and I were alone together. At times I would offer a statement defending my dad, but would just as quickly drop it if it seemed to upset her. Although I

secretly blamed her for my dad's drinking, this censure remained unspoken. What also went unspoken was the tremendous discomfort with my father when he later showed up. I had
the sense that in some unfathomable way I had betrayed him.

One way I could avoid dealing with my own feelings was
to focus on hers and try to make her feel better. Since it seemed
to work a lot of the time—she often did feel better when I gave
her attention—I drew the conclusion that I was not to focus
on my own feelings when I was with a woman; if I was nice
enough I could somehow magically fix her up and make her feel
better.

In the earliest stages of our relationship with mother, there
is an intense closeness that is actually appropriate. She carried
you as an embryo and as a fetus, so you were an inseparable
part of her body until you were born. Once you were born you
were still rhythmically and vibrationally attached to her and in
sync with her. During infancy there is a healthy symbiosis, where
infant and mother operate very much as a single unit.

If mother attempts to maintain the symbiosis beyond infancy by encouraging her son to have an unhealthy dependency
on her, he will feel the pinch of her need. As he grows, this
dependency on mother needs to be shed, ideally encouraged by
mother and supported by father. In optimal, healthy development, somewhere around the age of ten to eleven years old,
mother creates some emotional distance between herself and
her son. In relating to him, she needs to be more respectful and
less nurturing. Father becomes even more active in drawing his
son out of the world of Woman/mother and into the world of
men, with the help of some other men from his "tribe." This
is the healthy wound of separation referred to earlier.

If mother is needy in an unhealthy way and father isn't
around to draw the young boy into the world of men (which
was true for most of us), this sets up a split in the boy. On the
one hand, he feels the tug of mother and his own need for
contact with her, and on the other he feels a natural urge to be
separate and autonomous, to identify himself as a male. Her
engulfing behavior is an unconscious effort on her part to dis-

courage the separation and keep her son attached to her. And it takes more than mother's willingness to make this separation—it takes other men to assist.

The boy will react to this maternal engulfing behavior with either compliance or rebellion. If compliant, he becomes a nice boy, selfless and pleasing, doing what he can to look good in mother's eyes, containing any urges to separate for fear of losing mother's love. If he never makes this clear separation, then when he grows into adulthood he will likely transfer this compliance onto a woman, doing his best to placate her and not let her be disappointed in him. All his life he will be driven to perform well and do whatever he has to do in order to avoid rejection or disapproval from a woman.

Yet this behavior is typically not without some accompanying sense of internal conflict. A boy may covertly rebel against engulfment by outwardly acting in ways that are pleasing to his mother while secretly acting out in sneaky ways that he knows would earn him his mother's disapproval. He may get good grades but at the same time experiment with drugs, or he'll set fire to ants while he cleans out the garage like his momma told him.

My way of handling my mother's engulfing behavior was to put on the good face for her while sneaking down the street to my friend's treehouse to smoke his grandfather's cigarettes. When I was twenty years old, I was still trying to play the good-boy routine for my mother. I lived with my girl friend for almost a year, but maintained a chaste pretense with my mother, deathly fearing that she would somehow find out. I was very sneaky about it, feeling guilty and ashamed, living a lie so that my mother would not find out about it and be upset and disapproving.

As an adult, however a man reacts to this engulfing behavior, he will not have a clear sense of self apart from the woman he is with. He will most likely continue to feel engulfed by his partner. He may grow to resent this over time, secretly blaming the woman for being too controlling, demanding, or otherwise powerful. One option for him is to remain distant with women and relate to them only as sex objects. Seduction and conquest are ways to enact his resentment and avoid dealing with his fear of being engulfed. I transferred my sneakiness with my mother to Susan. I acted the part of the good husband while having affairs. In that way I acted out my resentment but did not risk engulfment, since I could always leave someone with whom I was having an affair. It was also a sneaky way to fight any engulfment patterns I felt with Susan, since if I maintained another relationship on the sly, she could never really "have" me.

Another way of acting out this resentment is by keeping not only distant, but quiet and passive. John has been married for forty-two years. He is a nice, passive man who has difficulty making eye contact when he talks. His body looks tired, as if he's been carrying a heavy weight for some time. During a workshop session on intimacy, he confessed, "I just don't get it. She keeps saying she wants me to tell her my feelings, but I don't always feel much. And whenever I do, she tells me there's something wrong with what I feel. There's no way to please her!" We could hear the years of pent-up frustration in his voice, years where he had adopted passivity as a strategy for dealing with an engulfing woman who was in many ways like his mother.

If a boy is overtly rebellious with this engulfing style of mothering, usually he will actively resist it. He may be the "problem child" of the family, avoiding any and all domination or intrusiveness by mother. Adolescence is typically a time when most males are touchy about being too close with mother anyway, so if a boy is actively resistant to this type of mothering, adolescence is when it will burst forth prominently. As he grows to be an adult, he may fiercely avoid entrapment by choosing to be with submissive women who do not challenge his fragile sense of autonomy. In the extreme, if a man is violent he may resort to rape or other forms of sexual acting-out in order to humiliate and get even with women. This type of behavior is a poor attempt to deny the engulfment, or to deny that Woman has any power over him at all.

ABANDONMENT

If it was a case of too little of mother, your mother was abandoning. Most of us to some degree have experienced engulfing behavior from mother, in part because of the absence of a strong father presence to provide a counterbalance. Some have more consistently experienced a mother who was emotionally unavailable, and was just not there in any substantial way. She may have been depressed or overwhelmed by the task of mothering, and undoubtedly she had poor mothering from her own mother. She may have been alcoholic or addicted to prescription drugs. Whatever the reasons, she wasn't there for you in ways that you needed her to be. Roger recalls, "She was drunk a lot of the time. I would come home from school and, nine times out of ten, she'd already had a couple of drinks. I could always tell because when I came home the television would be on full blast and she'd be on the couch with a glass in her hand. From as early as I can remember I'd have to get my sister fixed up for school because my mother would be sleeping one off. Dad wasn't much help. He just kind of ignored the whole thing and went about his business."

If your mother was abandoning, then as an adult it has been hard for you to form healthy attachments to a woman. The result is usually one of extremes. You may find that you don't get involved at all, in part because you have no precedent for being close to a woman. Jerome is twenty-eight years old, clean cut, polite, and lonely. He describes his mother as having been depressed as far back as he can remember, and doesn't remember her ever holding him or hugging him. He has never had an adult relationship with a woman. "There was one girl in high school that I liked, and I thought she liked me. It turns out she was just using me to make her ex-boyfriend jealous. I'd really like to have a girl friend now, but I'm just really shy around girls. There's one girl at work that's been pretty friendly and I'd like to ask her out, but I just don't know if she'd want to go out with me." Jerome's shyness has been his way of dealing with the wound of a mother who was unavailable; it is a wound that continues to interfere with his establishing a relationship with a woman today.

Another possible consequence of the wound of abandonment is that if you do get involved in a relationship, you keep yourself aloof and unavailable. Or you may have a series of partners, with the primary focus being sexual. This keeps you from facing the pain of potential abandonment from your partner. As long as you don't get too involved, too close, then you can't get hurt. Mario's mother raised him and his brother by herself, Mario's father having left before he was walking. "She was gone a lot. There was a string of men that she'd gotten involved with, and when there was a man in her life, that was it. She'd forget about me and my brother. She left us home by ourselves a lot." As an adult Mario has jumped from one sexual conquest to another. "I don't know what it is, but I start feeling real crowded after I've been with a woman for a couple of months. I keep thinking she's going to leave me, that there's another man. Sometimes crazy, paranoid stuff. So I jump the gun on her. You know what they say, the best defense is a good offense. So I leave and move on to the next one." Mario's distancing belies the great pain of his abandonment.

Another possible consequence of having an abandoning mother is that you yourself become engulfing, out of fear of being abandoned. You cling to your partner, motivated by the deep fear that if you don't stay close by she will leave you, just like mother left you. This clinging may be very passive or may be outright bullying, but either way it is controlling. It is an attempt to avoid the same feelings of abandonment you felt with your first woman, your mother. Ironically, the very thing you fear—abandonment— may result from your engulfing behavior.

Randy is recovering from a recent divorce. He was married for sixteen years to a woman who, in his words, "was a real bitch. She never seemed happy being at home. I made enough money for her to not have to work, but she said she had to do it. I mean, I can understand her need to get out of the house, but why work when you don't have to? I gave her everything she needed." Randy's clinging was demonstrated in his attempts to control his wife's every move. His anger covers the hurt he feels at what he sees as her abandonment, very much like what he experienced with his mother.

Exercise 25: Mother Engulfment/Mother Abandonment

In your journal write a description of your mother. Pay special attention to the ways in which she was engulfing and abandoning. What was she like when you were very small? When you were a young boy? An adolescent? Was she primarily abandoning? Engulfing? Or, as is often the case, a combination of the two? Was she different at different times in your life? Did she behave differently toward other siblings in your family? If so, how? If she is still living, what is she like now? What feelings surface for you as you write about this? Read this to another man, or in your men's group.

Gregory writes: "My mother seemed to be both engulfing and abandoning at different times. She was cold and distant much of the time—I don't remember her holding me or hugging me much at all—so I guess she was abandoning in that way. On the other hand, she was also very strict and protective. I know she was even more so when I was a teenager—I think it was hard for her to let me grow up. We used to argue all the time once I started high school, usually over things like how late I could stay out. She seemed a lot easier on my younger brother— I thought she let him get away with murder. Now, she's still distant a lot of the time, but I don't have all that much to do with her, so it doesn't bother me."

A portion of an entry from Raymond's journal: "My mother was very much engulfing. Since I was an only child and dad wasn't around much, I had to bear the brunt of her own feelings of being trapped. I dealt with it by becoming passive, which is the way I am with women these days. I think I learned to be more abandoning. That's what my last girl friend told me, in those words, 'You abandon me a lot.' I think that I learned to be passive as a way for my mother not to get to me, and now I'm doing the same damn thing with women today."

There are other kinds of wounds you may have received from your mother. Some of these are discussed below.

EMOTIONAL CRUELTY

Someone once said to me, "Boys will use fists to hurt, whereas girls will use words." If your mom used words, then you know that words can hit as hard as a fist. When I say emotional cruelty, I'm not talking about the occasional harsh words. Instead it's the systematic use of words to make you feel guilty and/or ashamed, putting you down and demeaning you constantly. It's your mother's attempt to control you by making you feel bad about yourself, her way of displacing all of her anger, rage, and frustration onto you through words that can sink deep into your psyche.

Whenever his mother was around him, Milt learned to tune her out. "She would constantly be talking, just like she was carrying on a one-way conversation. There wasn't a whole lot of opportunity to talk *with* her; it was more that she would talk *to* you. I think she was just lonely, with my dad working all the time. The point is, she could say the meanest things, and act like she didn't even know she had hurt me. One time I had a friend over and she was chattering away with this story about how, when I was smaller and was taking a bath, what a little penis I had. I was never more embarrassed in my life. My friend never let me live that one down."

If your mother put you down with words and you didn't feel you had a way to fight back, you had to hold in a lot of your hurt and anger you felt toward her. This likely carries over into your relationships with women today in the form of an undertone of hostility in your interactions. You may express it overtly by derogatory comments made to the woman you are with or else act it out through raging at her or with the more subtle passive-aggressive behavior. Milt continues, "Barbara, my girl friend, tells me I'm a rage-aholic. I don't like the label, but it's probably true. I don't know what happens, but sometimes I just lose it. Like the other night I came home, she said hello, and I really jumped her. I got pissed off because she had parked in my space in the driveway. From there I went on to about a million other things that were wrong, and she ended up running from the room. I don't understand what comes over me. I really don't want to hurt her, but I can see how I'm driving her away."

NOT BEING SEEN OR HEARD

Although this overlaps some of the other forms of wounding, I include this one because it is often a more subtle form of injury. If your mother was engulfing or abandoning, or as in Milt's case, emotionally abusive, she really didn't see or hear who you really are. If you were teased when you cried, then you concluded that it wasn't okay to express hurt when you felt hurt. If mother was abandoning, she did not provide a mirror for you or your feelings so that you got some validation for these natural expressions. If she demeaned you for expressing joy and happiness, you learned to hide those away as well. If she didn't hear your no when you were setting boundaries, even if you did so in a crude and rough fashion as most toddlers do, then you learned not to respect your own boundaries. If she suffocated you with her love, she couldn't see you, but acted only from her own need. Granted that others contributed to this, mainly father and siblings, but in the earliest formative years, mother was a primary influence.

If this was the case for you, then you've learned to expect that from women in your adult life. You may continually seek their validation and approval, never feeling quite sure of who you are unless you get a nod from a woman. This habit puts you in the position of never feeling okay about yourself, never feeling worthwhile unless you have the love of a woman. Oddly enough, you may have attracted as partners women who were not supportive or validating, thus re-creating the dynamics of the original relationship with mother.

Harold described how this happened for him with a woman

he had been dating: "She was bright, witty, and lots of fun, but as we got closer, she seemed to get more remote. I thought it was me—and I know some of it was—but I think that's just the way she was. She didn't talk about her feelings that much—kept them to herself. One night I opened up to her about how I really cared for her, and that I was feeling scared. She listened, thanked me for telling her, but didn't have much else to say. So I clammed up, and from there pretended that everything was fine. The truth is, it hurt a lot to put myself out there, and all she did was thank me for saying what I said! It seems like I get attracted to women who are remote like that. Maybe just bad luck." Or maybe he is playing out a pattern begun with his mother and isn't used to being seen or heard by a woman.

PHYSICAL ABUSE

Physical punishment was an acceptable means to deal with children in preceding generations. It was the common belief that you had to destroy the will of the child and the number-one priority was to teach him to obey. One way for a mother to do this was to use slappings and beatings when the child "got out of line." Never mind that this sort of abuse leaves emotional as well as physical scars. When you were a boy, she got away with it a lot more easily than when you grew to be stronger as a teenager.

"My mother used to beat us all the time," recalls Victor. "Really bad sometimes, too. She'd just fly off the handle about anything, and you couldn't tell when she would do it. When I was about fourteen, she came after me with a broomstick. I grabbed it from her and took it and broke it against the kitchen counter. Then I raised my fist and had the broken broomstick in my other hand and told her never to hit me again. She didn't. My dad kicked my ass when he got home, but she never tried to hit me again after that."

With a mother who was physically abusive, as an adult you may have either identified with your mother (and/or father) and become emotionally or physically abusive in your relationships with women, or you continued to identify yourself as the victim and have been on the receiving end of emotional and/or physical abuse from a woman. You either found yourself in relationships where you dominated, sometimes through your physical strength, or you let yourself be dominated. Victor's scar from the abuse still exists in the ways that he admittedly has treated his wife. "There's been only one time I actually hit her, early in the marriage, but she still remembers it. Mostly what I do though is yell at her a lot. I can see how hurt she has been by some of the things I've said. I guess I can get pretty mean when I'm angry. She finally packed her bags and moved out. That's what brought me into counseling."

SEXUAL ABUSE

More men are coming to the fore these days with descriptions of their sexual abuse as children. Typically the stories that we are hearing about and are making it to "Donahue" are the more horrific kinds of sexual abuse. Men are fortunately coming out of the dark to share their tales about fathers, stepfathers, uncles, and other guardians taking advantage of them sexually at an age when they didn't feel they had a right to say no. I fully support men in discovering and debriefing themselves of these personal horror stories, yet what has received little attention are the more subtle forms of sexual abuse.

Although typically this kind of sexual abuse is not as obvious or overt as others, a mother can sexually abuse her son as well. She may have her son sleep with her when he is old enough for this to be confusing to him. She may be seductive with him, or may be outright physically stimulating. The sexual abuse may be entirely emotional and nonphysical. In the instance of Milt, described above, the demeaning of his maleness is clearly sexually abusive. Teasing a boy as he goes through puberty, or putting down the pleasure that a boy will naturally feel in his body, is sexually abusive.

I recall when I was seven years old deciding one night to sleep in the nude. Ordinarily I slept in pajamas, but I wanted to experiment with this to see how it felt. I also felt very guilty about this, because I had never done it before and I wasn't sure my mother would approve. At bedtime I hid my pajamas under my pillow and climbed into bed, pulling the sheets up tight around me, so my mother wouldn't notice. I thoroughly enjoyed the sensual feeling of my skin against the sheets and briefly wondered what could possibly be wrong with doing this. My mother came in to tuck me in and say good night. I must have looked guilty or else had the sheets pulled up too tightly. My mother slipped her hand under the sheets, touched me on the hip, and as she did so she clucked her tongue and smiled. Giving me a sideways look, she said half-mockingly, half-seriously, "Steven! You're not wearing anything!"

I was embarrassed and ashamed, and yet at the same time her touch felt strangely arousing. She didn't say anything more after that, but I concluded that I was wrong for having gone to bed without my pajamas. She said good night, left the room, but my eyes were wide open. I lay there for the longest time, considering my options. Since I was a good momma's boy, I quietly slipped back into my pajamas, vowing that I would never do that again and risk such embarrassment. This and other instances of shaming around sexuality led me to feel very awkward and self-conscious about my body and my sexuality well into adulthood. I suspect that a lot of my sexual compulsiveness was a way to prove that I was okay.

Sexual abuse by mother can often set the stage for sexual addiction, where you become obsessed with sex or else act it out in some kind of compulsive manner. One man I know discovered that his compulsive exhibitionism was rooted in his mother's way of demeaning him sexually while at the same time walking around the house nude in such a way that he would see her. This provocative manner of displaying her sexuality occurred at a time in his development when he was especially susceptible to sexual arousal. If this kind of erotic tension existed between you and your mother, you could feel it, yet were forbidden to act on it or even acknowledge it in any way. This may have primed you for being sexually compulsive with a number of different women as a means of acting out the forbidden desire.

Exercise 26: Mother Wounds

In your journal, write more about the kinds of mothering you got. Did you receive any of these types of wounds we have been discussing? Was your mother emotionally abusive? Did she call you names or put you down a lot? Did she hit you or beat you? Do you feel that your mother really knew you? Did she hear you? Was there any overt or covert sexual abuse from her? How did she express her love—if she did? What kind of mothering did you need from her that you didn't get? How are your relationships with women similar to the one with your mother?

After you've written about this, read it to a man friend or to your men's group. After you've read it to another man, read this and your response to Exercise 25 to a woman you're close to—such as your wife, girl friend, or sister—and get their feedback.

Allen writes: "My mother didn't hit me and wasn't particularly mean with words, but the more I thought about this idea of covert sexual abuse, the more I could see how my mother was that way. She was really seductive, such as 'accidentally' letting me see her naked when I was a teenager. When she did, she would act uncomfortable but be smiling the whole time. And she would make these suggestive remarks about her body that I didn't quite know how to take but which made me feel embarrassed and uncomfortable. On the surface it looked rather innocent, but now I can see that there was this sexual charge to it, a combination of it being exciting and forbidden at the same time. I think this has had a lot to do with my sexual addiction—my trying to seduce women all the time. I haven't known how else to relate to women except sexually."

FOR THE LOVE OF MOTHER

Your mother contributed to your woundedness, sometimes directly, sometimes indirectly, and by so doing helped shape your present relationships with women. She also may have provided instances where she was loving, nurturing, and empathic. There were times when she held you, or cared for you when you were sick. If you had experiences like these with your mother, where she gave to you affectionately, then these memories are in your mind and body. It is this kind of love and caring, this feminine affection that we still seek from women today. And it is a unique and wonderful experience to be generously loved by a woman.

Yet because we have also had difficulties separating from Woman/mother, to seek this kind of love and caring cleanly and directly is virtually unheard of. Our need for this love tends to get distorted by our fears of losing ourselves in the fold of Woman/mother. Given this fear of losing ourselves, coupled with the obsessive preoccupation with sex that is a reaction to the tremendous repression in our culture, what many of us do is to sexualize our need for affection. In other words, whenever there is a need for touch or some physical loving, we translate that into lust. I suspect it also has to do with the attitude that we're real wimps if we need anything other than sexual touching with a woman.

This way of handling the need for affection also stems from the difficulties most of us have had in making a clean break from mother. If we relate to a woman via our need for pure affection there is a vague discomfort that we feel because it is reminiscent of mother's love; therefore it sparks any conflicts we may have about mother and our separation from her. Through sex, we can justify our need for caress and touch, because it is the "manly" thing to do. No wonder a lot of men spend so much time preoccupied with sex. This preoccupation is in part a masked expression of a much-neglected need for human touch.

Exercise 27: Receiving Mothering

While we may no longer need mother the way we once did, we always need mothering—pure, simple, nonsexualized affection from a woman. To help you experience what this is like, this exercise has two steps.

For the first step, close your eyes and imagine a woman you are close to. This could be your wife, sister, lover, or a woman friend. Imagine asking her to hold you. Now imagine her actually holding you. Notice your body's sensations. How is she holding you? What emotions do you notice? What do you want from her during this time of being held? What are you aware of about her body? Notice your sensations and notice how the physical contact feels with her. What fears do you notice? Does this provoke any memories, good or bad, of being held by a woman?

For the next step, actually ask the woman you have in mind to hold you. This may be a bit of a stretch, particularly if you have not had any experience of being held like this, except perhaps when you've been sexual with a woman. It can be frightening, and if this is so, observe how you deal with your fears and apprehension. Do you try to sexualize it or act seductive? Do you make a joke of it? Do you focus on her and worry about how she is doing? Observe yourself from planning to actual experience, and do your best to relax into the experience. As always during these types of exercises, pay close attention to what's going on in your body. Breathe deeply and slowly throughout. Write about your experience in your journal. Especially note any differences between imagining that you are receiving mothering from a woman and how you feel when you are actually doing so.

When I asked my friend Marilyn to hold me, I wasn't feeling particular sexual, nor did I have the need to act sexual with her. It was difficult asking her, but she consented. I crawled into her arms and she cradled me. It felt wonderful, but at first it was hard to relax. I kept thinking that she must be getting tired of it or she must not really want to do this. I kept trying to take care of her, checking with her to see if she was okay, if I was too heavy. This is the same kind of feeling that I had with my mother, that I couldn't relax and just receive from her without having to do something to comfort or take care of her. Marilyn finally said, "Look, I'm fine. Just relax and let me hold you. You don't have to do anything." My mother patterning had been triggered, just as yours will be when you experiment with letting yourself be held.

So from this first relationship with a woman, mother, you have set some patterns that you have maintained into the present day. It is not only that mother has wielded her influence, it is the incredible power of the feminine that you first encountered with mother.

THE POWER OF THE FEMININE

Through most of our lives we have sought, reacted to, resented, resisted, cherished, surrendered to or have otherwise been obsessed with the feminine. I say "the feminine" because even though we first encountered it in our mothers, it isn't just mother, wife, lover, or a woman that we have to confront and deal with throughout our lives. It is the feminine principle, which is found to some degree in any and all of these women. It represents that which is soft, receptive, emotional, intuitive, sensual, dark, moist, elusive, witchy, moody, nurturing, connected, relational, and hard to grasp or define in any linear fashion.

We are alternately attracted to this force and fearful of it. The ongoing attempts to reconcile this dilemma are characterized by how our relationships with women are played out in our lives. The power of the feminine is the mystery of creation that we see embodied in a woman, an intimacy with nature that allows her to birth new life through her body. For most men there is something incredibly awesome and miraculous about this.

Robert Lawlor in *Earth Honoring* goes so far as to say (italics his),

> *I believe every male, whatever his type or season of life, whether he be heterosexual, homosexual or bisexual, lives through, and for, the love of the feminine. That woman, or feminine principle, can be within another male, within himself, or an external female. A man furthers his own life and destiny when he furthers the life and destiny of the women, or woman, he loves.*

There are powerful words for a powerful principle. The feminine is the object of our love, curiosity, admiration, and envy.

As men, we can express our creativity in other physical and mental ways through our works, but we will never really know what it's like to gestate and give birth to a new human being through our bodies. I think we are continually in awe of the creative power of the feminine, and perhaps our efforts to create via the material of the earth are poor attempts at mimicking her natural power.

We both fear and revere the feminine. Starting with mother and our own differentiation, there is the contrasting desire to merge with the feminine and the opposite drive to be independent from it/her. One way I can express this conflict is through "the metaphor of the toilet seat." My second wife successfully trained me to put down the toilet seat after I peed. Not only did my wife want this, but I had two girls as offspring, and when they were ready to be potty trained, I was sure they would appreciate it as well. After my separation and divorce, I was so habituated to this action that I usually put the toilet seat down immediately after the last drop without thinking about it.

One day I caught myself in the act. Here I was, living alone in a house where I had my own bathroom, and I was still putting the toilet seat down. Why? I puzzled with this for a few moments, and in a daring act of rebellion, I reached down and put the toilet seat back up. I felt a certain strength of resolve while doing this. It was a supreme, symbolic "Fuck you!" to my ex-wife, and in some way, to all women who I thought were trying to control me. The triumphant feeling soon passed, however, and gave way to a feeling that this was rather childish, so I just as quickly reached out and put the toilet seat back down. It did look much more aesthetically appealing and it made less noise when you flushed it, plus things wouldn't fall into it when the lid was down. No sooner had I replaced the seat in its down position than I again questioned my motives. I was caught in the trap of questioning whether I was still doing this just to please a woman, or did it in fact make more sense to leave it down? So I reached out again and put the seat back up in its wide-open position, turned around, and marched out of the room before I could think about it any longer. Alas, it wasn't that easy. For several minutes after that, I obsessed about the pros and cons of my action. At this point in my life it seems quite irrelevant, but for a few brief moments it encapsulated my struggle with Woman.

Because in our culture there has usually not been a clear demarcation from mother and a formal entry into the world of men, we have spent much of our lives reacting to the feminine, trying to deny it, control it, own it, please it, or demean it. Since the task of separation was not handled during adolescence or young adulthood, to heal the wounds regarding relationships with women, we must first make a clean break with mother and learn about ourselves as men before we can enter into relationships with women feeling a security and an appreciation for our manhood.

GOOD-BYE MOTHER, HELLO MANHOOD

One of the main tasks in moving from boyhood to manhood is separating from mother and moving into the world of men. This wound of separation from mother, which must take place if a boy is to become a man, may hurt, and the boy may grieve the sense of loss with mother. Yet it is a healthy wound, one that

sets up the move into the world of men. Since there have typically not been any prescribed rituals to provide this, now as an
adult you can make a conscious decision to do so. Sam Keen,
in *Fire in the Belly*, puts it quite succinctly. "To be free from
and for women, to discover the unique ground of manhood, a
man must take leave of Motherland."

If you didn't make the separation from your mother during
adolescence, which is true for most of us, then it is something
you must do now as an adult. If she has died there are still ways
that you can actively separate from her, such as the good-bye
letter described later in this section. If she is still alive you may
make the break all at once by letting your mother know you
will not be seeing her, or you may do it in stages. It is a matter
of your setting boundaries and being willing to let her disap-
prove of you or even outright reject you. I remember a few years
ago I confronted my mother and told her the truth rather than
acting out the role of her comforter and caretaker. She had
called complaining about my dad's drinking, as usual.

As she started complaining, I interrupted her and said,
"Mom, I don't want to hear this. I'm really tired of hearing
you complain about Dad's drinking. There's nothing I can do
about it."

"What do you mean?" she asked.

"Just what I said. Whenever Dad goes on one of his binges,
you call me and complain to me, and I don't want to hear it
anymore. Go to Al-Anon. Call the union. We talked about the
programs they have for alcoholism. Get a counselor or someone
you can talk to. I refuse to take the role with you anymore. Dad
may drink himself to death, and you can't stop him. But you
can do something for yourself."

There was very little conversation after that. I heard
through my brother that she was very upset with me. I didn't
talk to her for a couple of months. Throughout this time, I
knew I did what I had to do. She didn't follow any of my
suggestions, but what she did do was stop complaining to me
about my father's drinking. I subsequently had a couple of other
confrontations with her about her continual complaints about

her physical symptoms and about her lack of interest in me and my life. Each time I felt stronger and less attached to pleasing her or avoiding her disapproval. This was one of the first steps for me in making that break from mother.

One way you can consciously let go of mother is to write a letter, specifically a letter saying good-bye to her. It may or may not mean that you are actually relinquishing all contact with her, although you may choose to do that as part of your process of maturing into manhood. Whether she is living or dead, writing this kind of a letter is one step in releasing her.

Exercise 28: Saying Good-bye to Mother

Write a letter saying good-bye to your mother. In it, include your anger, hurt, fears, regrets, and any love that you may feel as you write it. Start it out stating that you are saying good-bye, that you are releasing her as your "mom," that you are a man now and don't need a mom or a momma anymore. Like the letter to dad, don't censor your feelings. Write whatever comes to you; let the wounded boy inside speak his piece. Write until you have nothing more to write, which may be one page or may be several.

If your mother is still alive, let the letter sit for a couple of days before deciding whether or not you want to give it to her. The more important part of this exercise is in the writing of the letter, not in giving it to your mother. If you do decide to give it to her, get ready. Don't expect her to be any different than she has been for most of your life. If she does react differently, such as opening up, look at that as an extra.

You can also write this type of letter if your mother is no longer living. Obviously you can't give it to her, but you can still benefit. It can help you sort through your feelings and ultimately put your relationship with her to rest. I'd suggest burning the letter in a ceremony of your own creation, then either tossing the ashes in the ocean or burying them.

You can repeat this exercise as many times as you need, each successive one being another step in letting go of mother. I will guarantee you that each time will be different. Sometimes the prominent feeling will be anger, sometimes sadness, sometimes tenderness and appreciation. Sometimes you will discover a whole range of feelings all in one setting. I suggest writing this letter about once every three months, or whenever you find that you feel especially angry, sad, or frustrated with women in your life, or if you are dealing with a particular issue with your mother.

I've written this type of letter on a few occasions, each time feeling less and less need for my mother's love and approval. The last time I wrote to her was shortly following her death just a couple of months ago. I'd had a chance to say my final good-bye in the hospital about one week before her death. This letter was written the night before her memorial service:

Dear Mom,

Here I sit on the eve of your memorial, tired, worn down, and nervous about being with all the family tomorrow. This family is funny about feelings. So many of us feel things deeply, but are so scared to show it. Yet lately I've been committed to telling the truth about who I am, and this includes what I'm feeling.

The truth about you. I feel sad that you never knew me. It was hard watching you slip away over the last couple of years. You lost so much of your vitality. I'm glad we said our good-byes a couple of weeks ago. You smiled when you saw me. You smiled. You really saw me. I wasn't just one of your sons. You saw me. That meant a lot.

And I told you it was all right to die, to let go. You seemed to understand. I assured you that Dad would be all right, and that I would look out for him.

I feel grateful that you died. You were hurting a

lot. It was hard for Dad to see you in so much pain, but just as hard to let you go. What was it like? Were you conscious when you breathed your last breath, your heart so weakened beat its final rhythm?

I still have a lot of pain and anger about our relationship that I need to simply feel. I will do this over time. You were not a perfect mother. I'm learning that I don't have to be a perfect son.

I've been saying the Lord's Prayer a lot when I think of you. Tonight is the first time I can feel your presence, your spirit.

Blessings be with you Mom. Good-bye. I love you.

                                                          Steven

The break from mother/Woman now as an adult need not be sudden or abrupt, nor will it necessarily come as a result of her death. Saying good-bye to mother, via the letter writing or in actuality taking a break from being in contact with her, are certainly effective ways. For most of us, being involved with other men on an ongoing basis will be another important step in not only severing the ties with mother and our enmeshment with Woman but also moving into the world of men. One effective way to do this is described in the following chapter on men's groups.

Another element of separating from mother/Woman is to learn to seek solitude, to be alone without distractions from the external world so that you can be deeply aware of what is going on inside you.

Exercise 29: Solitude

Step 1: Spend a stretch of unscheduled time alone. For example, take one day this coming weekend. Ask for your family's cooperation in giving you a gift of an entire day—or at the very least several hours—to yourself. Be aware of a likely temptation

to schedule the time with a lot of things to do. All the things
you think you have to do can wait. Keep reminding yourself
of this constantly. In taking this time for yourself, unplug the
phone, don't watch television—just spend quiet time with
yourself. Keep your journal at your side and do a lot of writing
in it about your thoughts, feelings, and observations. Go for
walks outdoors, perhaps in a nearby park. Do a lot of slow,
deep breathing, paying attention to all the sensations and feelings in your body. Notice anything that gets in the way of
purely enjoying this time, and continue to remind yourself to
relax.

Step 2: Plan and then take your next vacation somewhere
alone where you can have a few days of solitude and reflection.
Although this may not be easy to do, it will introduce you to
any barriers you may have to solitude. When you do, avoid any
distractions such as alcohol, drugs, sex, television, or the telephone. Read, write, meditate, and walk a lot. Any time you
spend in solitude can be valuable. These are steps you must
take to clarify your identity as a man, from the inside out, and
to touch into a deeper spiritual reality of who you are. In your
solitude write every day in your journal. Note especially any
feelings of fear, sadness, or grief. There is a dark passage through
loneliness to get to a place of solitude. As Rainer Maria Rilke
says in *Letters to a Young Poet*, "What is necessary, after all, is
only this: solitude, vast inner solitude. To walk inside yourself
and meet no one for hours—that is what you must be able to
maintain."

Scott took a backpacking trip by himself for four days recently. Although he has been backpacking before, this was the
first time he'd gone by himself. He reports, "I had nothing to
distract me. The first couple of days I walked a lot, partly because I didn't want to slow down and think about being by
myself. After the first two days I slowed down and took lots of
stops. I went into this whole other space that's difficult to describe. I was very aware of my aloneness, yet at the same time
very aware of my connection with nature. I felt like my senses

were incredibly alert. This may sound strange, but I was even communicating with some of the animals along the way! It was an incredible experience."

As you experience yourself increasingly separate from mother such that you neither have to feel trapped by your need for her love and approval nor react in opposition to prove that you don't need her, you will begin to see how some of the dissatisfactions you have with women are related to the wounds you got from mother. As you become more aware of these patterns in your present relationships you will then have a chance to change these patterns.

There will be many opportunities for you to interact with women in your own healing journey. As you do, I can't stress enough how important it is to continue to shore up your associations with men, to deepen these friendships spiritually and emotionally, and to attempt to meet more of your needs both through these friendships and by going more deeply inside yourself. Through these experiences you can continue to clarify your sense of yourself as a man, which will set the stage for richer and more creative relationships with women. To encourage these kinds of relationships you must challenge in yourself any rigid stereotypes about what it is to be a man, including your macho act as well as your sensitive male act, and instead let your "wild man," your instinctual voice, be heard, felt, and outwardly expressed. This will be especially true in any partnerships you have or will develop with other women.

This way of thinking about relationships contradicts what has been typically true in our society. Traditionally, men and women have treated each other as objects, specifically as sex objects, but in gender-specific ways. Men have looked at women as beauty objects, while women have looked to men as success objects, often forming relationships based on these characteristics.

Sex Objects: Success And Beauty

The media tantalizes us as adolescents and young men by bombarding us with images of voluptuous females who support the fantasy of a certain ideal female, a "10," that in truth falls within a very narrow range of feminine beauty. These images, such as the women in the men's magazines, set a precedence for adolescent fantasies. Women become beauty objects. For the vast majority of us, this type of female is in reality unattainable, yet the fantasy prevails.

As I've talked with other men about earlier fears and experiences, I found that while the details of each of our stories varied, we had a lot in common. Most of us have experienced fantasies and desires for the unattainable female, and most of us have discovered that you have to be a successful performer in some way in order to be desirable to a female. In *Why Men Are the Way They Are*, Warren Farrell has identified and elaborated on some of the dilemmas we have with the opposite sex.

For centuries, women have been trained to repress their sexual energies and redirect them to finding emotional and financial security for themselves and for their children. In order to do so, a woman has had to be sexually desirable but remain somewhat aloof. She must present her sexuality yet deny access to it at the same time. She is holding on to her "primary fantasy" of catching a male who will protect her and provide her with financial and emotional security, and her sexuality is used as barter for the fulfillment of this fantasy.

Reciprocally, our training as men has taught us that in order to achieve the "prize" of the sexual favors of the desired woman, we have to compete. To be competitive, we must perform, continually proving ourselves as men, first in high school, then in our careers, so that a woman who is desirable will become our sexual partner. This is a man's primary fantasy: to have access to as many women as possible without rejection. In order to do so, we must become what Farrell calls "success objects." The problem is that once we have proven ourselves and achieved the "prize," we come up against the female's hidden agenda: What she really wants is a provider and protector. If she is successful in enacting her agenda, the male will compromise his primary fantasy and adapt to her criteria for a mate. Even though he has gotten his prize, he never really gets the fantasy.

Because of this emphasis on competition and striving, which are a man's part in the sexual drama, to a greater degree he must deny certain essential aspects of himself that are so fundamentally human. As Robert Lawlor says in *Earth Honoring*,

> This repression of femininity, combined with the male pattern of pressure to compete on a nonsexual level for sexual favors, tends to generate imbalance in the psychological state of the "typical male." Under the pressures of constant competition, a man tends to lose his capacity to express his feelings and needs. He is not allowed to be afraid and is ill prepared to accept failure. His obsessions with success, assertiveness, and performance leave him unable to be receptive, passive, playful, and sensual—in other words, human.

From the earliest stages of our budding sexuality, we have learned to look at competition and success as that which will yield the prize of the beautiful, sexual female. This attitude prevails in Western culture, sustained by commercial advertising that caters to what is essentially an adolescent male fantasy.

No wonder we as men have had so much difficulty in relationships with women. As long as we maintain all the attitudes and behaviors that support competition and success in order to gain and maintain the female of our desire, we will pay in terms of our relationships and our ability to be playfully and passionately alive. We not only treat women as objects, we treat ourselves as objects. A woman becomes a sex/beauty object; we become sex/success objects. In a relationship with a woman, we find it difficult to feel and act in ways that will contradict this training.

Norm was by any standards a success. He had worked hard

to create his company from the ground up. In fact his hard work had been one of the factors in the break-up of his first marriage. Now in his second marriage, to a very pretty woman named Sharon, after three years he started hearing complaints from her that were similar to those he had heard from his first wife. "Liz [Norm's first wife] used to say to me how I wasn't there very much, but with Liz I didn't particularly want to be around anyway. Sharon was complaining that I wasn't around much, so I changed my schedule so I could be at home more because I do want to be with her. The only problem is that I still have to work at least one or two nights late in the office to get done what I have to get done. Lately she's been complaining that I don't talk to her as much as I used to. I usually don't have much to say, but I'm happy to listen to her."

Like a lot of men, Norm has difficulty balancing all the traits that have helped him be as successful as he is with the characteristics that are needed for a sustained intimate relationship with a woman. It is a common dilemma, one that has no easy solutions. Success in a man is attractive to most women, yet the very behaviors needed for success can interfere with developing and nurturing relationships. It becomes its own trap wherein isolation is the fruit of our achievements.

Gary and his wife, Sylvia, have been married for nineteen years, living separately the last several months. They are working on reconciliation, and Gary is realizing how his achievement orientation has cost him in many ways, but particularly with regard to his relationships with his wife and three children. "I'd spend ten to twelve hours at the office, talking with people, calling this person or that, running meetings, having business lunches, and by the time I'd get home I wouldn't want to deal with *anything*. I'd walk in the door and my wife would say hello and I would immediately find fault with her greeting. My kids would want to be with me, and all I wanted to do was be alone for a while. If I slowed down at all I'd feel exhausted, and sometimes I'd end up falling asleep almost as soon as I sat down. We grew further and further apart as a result. Now I'm living by myself, and I'm still doing the same routine. When I get the chance to be alone, I want to work because I don't like being alone that much."

For both Norm and Gary, the shortcomings of their chosen role model are painfully evident. To continue to relate rigidly to oneself as a success object, although it may have had something to do with the initial attraction from the woman, leads down a dangerous path. It leaves very little room for a man to connect with his core of being and discover there his innate wildness and tenderness of spirit. The answer lies certainly not in playing out the game of objectifying either oneself or one's partner, nor will it be found in totally denying the reality of this system as it stands.

Since this kind of stereotyping is so widespread, there aren't any simple solutions. Through the kind of awareness that quite naturally develops when you make a commitment to heal your woundedness, you will most likely find that you simply lose interest in treating yourself solely as a success object and in treating a woman only like a beauty object. Since much of this healing process is internal and interpersonal, the insights you will be discovering will lend themselves to a more diverse way of being with yourself—and, in turn, of being with a woman.

Exercise 30: Role Reversal

This exercise is designed to increase your awareness of the kind of stereotyping that we do with ourselves and with women. Tell a woman friend, your wife, or lover about the journey you've been on while reading this book. Ask her if she would be willing to do an exercise in role reversal with you. If she agrees, then proceed. Plan to go out on a date, pretending it is a first date, only switch traditional roles completely from planning the date to the actual date. Play it out all the way; do not drop your reversed roles until the evening is finished. She must make the arrangements, come and pick you up, and generally be the one to initiate. You must be receptive, a bit seductive but not too available. Definitely do not make the first moves. If the two of you are already sexual with one another and you want to carry through, you can include lovemaking as part of the evening. If you do, once again, be more receptive than initiating. Give yourselves at least one day to reflect on your experience of the evening, and during that time write about it in your journal. Afterward, talk with each other about your experience.

Leon tried this with a woman friend, Martha. "She and I had a great time with this one. The hardest thing about it was keeping in character. I found myself going back and forth between doing 'womanly' things and doing my usual routine as a man. For instance, Martha kept putting the moves on me through most of the evening. I had a hard time acting disinterested, since we'd agreed ahead of time that the evening wouldn't end up in our having sex. Especially as we were riding home, she kept putting her hand on my leg. I got kind of turned on, but I stayed in character. She never got to first base."

Beyond Macho: Sensitivity Training

While there are still men who clamor for the holy grail of fame and fortune and therefore find themselves trapped in the ranks of those who feel like "success objects," there are others who, in their search for something different than this industrial age stereotype, have tried going the route of sensitivity.

As I previously stated, in the 1970s, perhaps in part as a reaction to the women's movement and the general interest in consciousness raising, many of us heeded the call to become more sensitive, more feeling, and to "express our feminine side." We learned to shed tears and become more open and vulnerable—at least with women. Sometimes it took the place of success as a means for capturing the prize of the woman's sexual favors, and provided a contemporary answer to the age-old question, "What do women really want?" Even though this new sensitivity was a reaction to what men supposed women wanted rather than an internal drive to truly feel and express more, it was the seed for us to develop our inner life and learn to pay attention to our feelings.

I recall thinking at that time, "Well, if that's what women want, okay. I'll learn to listen more closely and share my feelings." I was already a good listener, a good friend women would and could look to for comfort and companionship. I had learned a long time ago to be a good listener and a source of comfort for my mother, so I had a head start at this. Yet much of the time I still felt as if I were acting the part rather than really feeling—I wasn't there. Sometimes this sensitive, nurturing persona worked to gain me sexual favors from the woman I was with. I was nonaggressive, pleasant, relatively easy to be with, yet I had very little sense of myself, of my own power and substance. Over the next few years I became increasingly gentle, attracting women who wanted a "sensitive male." In performing this role, however, I neglected an important dimension of myself as a man. I had little clarity about who I was or what direction I was going in. I had learned to "handle" women by always trying to please them, and in doing so I remained undefined with women except insofar as how I reacted to what I thought they wanted from me.

From Macho To Fierce Lover

This foray into expressing our feminine side was a necessary step in our evolution. It was a polar opposite to the macho image and therefore less outwardly damaging and disconnected. Yet in many instances it was just so much mush. That wild spirit, the deeper masculine energy, was missing. By becoming the sensitive male, we turned inward, learned to be more caring, compassionate, and loving, but our energy became flat and constrained.

In *Iron John*, Robert Bly commented on what he termed the "soft" male:

> They had learned to be receptive, but receptivity wasn't enough to carry their marriages through troubled times.

In every relationship something *fierce* is needed once in a while. Both the man and the woman need to have it. But at that point when it was needed, often the young man came up short. He was nurturing, but something else was required—for his relationship, and for his life.

The "soft" male was able to say, "I can feel your pain, and I consider your life as important as mine, and I will take care of you and comfort you." But he could not say what he wanted, and stick by it. *Resolve* of that kind was a different matter.

This type of resolve does not eliminate gentleness and sensitivity, but embraces these qualities along with a sense of inner conviction and fiery determination. This is the passion of being in touch with the wild man. In our woundedness we have lost touch with this quality of fierceness and instead have adopted stereotypes, whether they be stereotypes of the successful or the sensitive male.

Ironically it took a woman initially to shake me out of this unconscious malaise, where I acted sensitive and didn't have the strength of resolve or conviction. I was without exception gentle, soft, and kind to women. Any and all of my rage was totally denied and repressed. With Katy, a woman I dated after my separation from my second wife, this was true. Aside from my being habitually cautious and careful with a woman so that I wouldn't hurt her, I was still reeling with a lot of guilt and shame from my separation, especially in that I was feeling incredibly responsible for my wife's emotional pain. Katy was a good-looking woman with a hard edge to her. At the time I first met her, she drove a motorcycle, dressed in the full regalia of helmet and leathers. It was actually very sexy. Leather has never seemed the same since.

She was also very sexually aggressive, to which I took no offense. We had been lovers a short while, and I was doing my best to be a good, gentle, compassionate lover, which is what I thought most women wanted. At one point we were making love, and Katy, in her charming, inimitable way, stopped the proceedings and looked me squarely in the eyes. She said, "Steven, a woman isn't *that* fragile. I'm not going to break, you know. You don't have to be so damned careful. Where's your passion? If you don't feel it, at least *act* like it's there—maybe then you'll start to feel it. Here. Like this." At which point she proceeded to ravish me aggressively. I got the message.

Although I was somewhat hurt and taken aback by the forcefulness and directness of what she said, I knew she was right. Something was missing. Not simply my aggressiveness, but the passion, the fierceness that would drive that aggressiveness. From here I experimented with being more aggressive with her. Although the first few times were tentative, I liked it. I initiated sex, rather than waiting for her to do so. With her encouragement and responsiveness I could feel my solidness as a man. Our sexual play became more creative and enjoyable. Though acted out in our lovemaking, through it all a great realization was beginning to dawn on me: I could be assertive with a woman and she wouldn't fall apart.

This was far different from what I had concluded while growing up and what was later reinforced in other relationships with women. Without being consciously aware of it, I had assumed that all women were helpless, fragile, and needy; my role with my female partner, as I saw it, was to be there for her, to listen to her, comfort her, and, if I could, to "fix" her when she was emotionally distraught. Just like mother.

This is what we men will inevitably do. We will take those characteristics of mother, project them onto the woman with whom we are involved, and, given enough time, relate to her in ways similar to how we related to mother. It doesn't mean that you consciously look for mother—in fact, you may find someone as opposite to your mother as possible—but simply that, eventually, you will begin reacting to this woman in ways that you used to react to mother. It's inevitable, but that doesn't mean we have to be trapped by our projections. The more aware you can become of these tendencies, the more likely it will be that you can break some of these habits.

Exercise 31: Mothers, Wives, and Lovers

Consider the woman with whom you are involved, or else your most recent past relationship. How is, or was, she like your mother? Not necessarily physical appearance, but in personality and her style of relating, and so on? How is she unlike your mother? How do you see yourself relating to her in ways you related to your mother? Do you let her be powerful? What buttons of yours does she push? Talk this over with a close male friend, someone who knows you and will give you honest feedback. After you talk this over with your male friend, discuss it with a female friend. See if her perspective on this is different from your man friend's. What did you learn from this? Write your observations in your journal.

I had never considered my former wife to be much like my mother, but with the advantage of hindsight I see the similarities (as well as the differences) much more clearly. They were both quite self-centered, angry, emotionally reactive, and tended to deny a lot of their sensuality. They were both dedicated to their children, each in her own way. I was very intimidated by closeness to either one, and tended to take a caretaking role with both. I denied a lot of myself with each, and tried my best to be ideal—an ideal son to my mother, an ideal husband to my wife. With both I found it next to impossible to meet my needs, typically because I didn't know what they were and, even when I did, I didn't ask for them to be met. These are but a few that I've so far spotted.

MEN AND WOMEN TOGETHER

In the process of our healing, you can come together with women in some truly generative ways. The more freedom you give yourself to be the man you are, the more freedom you can give to your partner to be the woman she is. The more you are willing to explore and discover, the more exciting and dynamic your relationships will be. This is true whether or not you are sexual with each other. Whether friends or lovers or friends *and* lovers, as you more consistently tell the truth about yourself in your journey of healing and discovery, as you make awakening your number-one priority, the more alive you will be and, in turn, the more alive will be your relationships with women.

As you take exploratory risks with women friends, it's helpful to note that aside from the obvious biological differences, there are some significant differences between the way that we as men tend to function and the way women will tend to operate. These differences are not faults, they are simply differences. When fully acknowledged, they can be complementary. For instance, you will not experience your feelings in the same way she does. She will be more intimately connected to her emotions, whereas you will be able to detach from your feelings more easily. This can be a strength and something you can bring to a relationship with a woman, just as her ability to swim in emotional waters can be an asset for both of you.

You will not see things in your relationship that she will see. The feminine principle in a woman is more acutely attuned to the relationship and relational subtleties. For me, when a woman friend senses something going on in our relationship and expresses it to me, I try to listen very closely because she is most often picking up on something intuitively that I am only faintly aware of, if at all. This sort of acuity can be very valuable for you.

On the other hand, you will be able to bring perspective into the relationship—not an unfeeling perspective, but one that can complement the woman's innate ability to be close to her feelings. When a woman is caught up in a maelstrom of emotion, from the deepest place of your own masculine power you can penetrate this with your own clarity and perspective. This does not mean that you are trying to control her or avoid your own feelings but that you are providing illumination to her innermost sensings.

A woman who is particularly aware and expressive of her own deeper feminine self can be quite bold and fiery, sometimes jarring us out of our nonfeeling detachment back into our emotions, awakening us from our reverie. When a woman is in tune with her own feelings and her feminine spirit, this kind of female energy can serve to keep us honest and in tune with our emotions.

Sometimes this is misinterpreted as bitchiness or hostility out of our own ego defensiveness and need to be in control. When it is disconnected from her deeper feminine spirit, it probably is bitchiness and complaint. Because a woman can often sense things that are going on in a relationship before we do, she may try to push us into seeing them also, or else try to manipulate us into going along with her version of the relationship. This could be a woman's "fatal flaw" since when a man feels pushed he will usually fight back, either quietly or outright aggressively. When a woman stubbornly tries to be right with a man, to force her point of view, she will get nothing but defensiveness from him. The lessons for a woman in relating to a man are to stay grounded in her emotional nature and her spirit, and to be patient. Because of our tendency toward detachment, we will typically be slow in getting the gist of what she is saying. I often advise a female client not to hold back with her husband or lover, but also to give him space to absorb what she has said. Sometimes a man has to go away and think about what his woman has said.

Because we are slow on the uptake when it comes to acknowledging the truth of what's going on in a relationship, our fatal flaw is to stubbornly close out everything that the woman is saying, and become distant and aloof. When we are involved in a relationship with a woman, most of us feel very protective toward her. I have no doubt that a man would without hesitation give up his life in order to protect his wife and his children. This protective aura gets misguided when a woman is communicating her feelings to us. Usually we feel like we have to do something with her feelings, or fix them in some way. More often than not, she is wanting to connect, and this is one of the best ways to do so, through communicating feelings. A simpler though sometimes difficult way to engage a woman who is sharing her feelings is not to feel responsible or think you have to make her feel better, but simply to listen. Since we are often oriented toward doing rather than being, this is frequently harder than it sounds.

Exercise 32: Man and Woman Together

With your spouse, lover, or close female friend, read through excerpts of this chapter that are pertinent for you and your relationship. Take your time in discussing and sharing with each other your responses. Let yourself feel any emotions that surface. How can you deepen your love and appreciation of each other? To do so, what fears or concerns does that bring up in you? Talk these over, not in some attempt to come to a conclusion, but simply to talk. You may do this over several sessions. Each time you have this kind of discussion, spend some time afterward writing about your responses in your journal.

As to the topic of relationships, John Welwood, Ph.D., in "The Wild Spirit of Male and Female," in the Fall 1990 issue of *Sacred Fire* magazine, summarizes it this way:

> Thus, consciously or unconsciously, we often try to domesticate our partners. Binding them to us and trying to make them fit our needs, we sever their connection to the roots of their power. A woman may give up her own separate friends, activities, and ways of being to please her man. Or a man may give up his solitude and

come to depend on his woman for vital energy. In so doing, they lose the wild otherness and beauty that attracted them to each other in the first place. What remains are two domesticated *persons* who have lost the vitality and mystery essential to sustain a vibrant love.

". . . a man and a woman can learn to guard and protect their own and each other's wildness. To do this, they must cultivate their own individual connection to the deepest powers of life, instead of primarily deriving their sense of aliveness from each other. Men and woman who are in touch with their native powers can help each other honor their free, elemental spirit in their everyday relations. They can become powerful allies, helping each other awaken to these larger powers.

This gives a general idea of what is possible as we proceed with our healing and bring what we discover into a relationship with a woman. Like the rest of your healing journey, it is a project that is never finished until you die. And, lest we forget, I recall the words of a friend of mine when I was weightily pondering and questioning the purpose of the relationship in which I was involved: "I think it should be to have fun!"

Next, I will give you some specifics on setting up an excellent resource for male energy: a men's group.

7

A Community of Men

INTO THE WORLD OF MEN

In some cultures there are formal rituals that the entire community enacts, initiations that take the young boy/adolescent from mother and teach him about what it takes to be a man in that culture. Usually it isn't the father, or only the father, but older men from the community who welcome the boy into the world of men through rituals, traditions, and stories that have been handed down for generations.

Robert Bly has spoken and written extensively about these traditions from other cultures. In *Iron John* he describes one that takes place amongst the Kikuyu in Africa, wherein the boy is taken from his mother to a place outside the village, where he fasts for three days. At the end of the three days he then sits with the older men around the campfire, scared and confused. Each man takes a knife and, one at a time, cuts himself, bleeds a little into a bowl, then passes the knife and bowl to the other men, who each do the same thing. When the bowl comes to the boy, he drinks from it. Bly comments:

> In this ritual the boy learns a number of things. He learns that nourishment does not come only from his mother, but also from men. And he learns that the knife can be used for many purposes besides wounding

195

others. Can he have any doubts now that he is welcome among the other males?

As colorful and as full of meaning as it is, this particular ritual would obviously not work in our culture. Yet we don't have any specific cultural rituals that initiate boys into manhood. Bar mitzvahs and fraternity initiations are the closest we come, yet these are pallid in comparison to the rich and diverse initiation rites of other cultures. Without these kinds of rituals and without older men to serve as spiritual mentors to initiate boys into the world of men, we are left continually uncertain about what it really means to be a man, with a resulting ambivalence in our relationships with women. To resolve this uncertainty we will have to do something in our adult lives not only to move *away* from the feminine, whether represented by mother, wife, or girl friend, but also to take steps to move *into* the world of men. Through doing so we can then go on to form genuinely creative partnerships with women. Without having been initiated, it's only as we let ourselves feel supported and validated by other men that we can become more secure and grounded in our identity.

The first step in this process is to go into the world of men, to make it a point to be with other men in deeper and more meaningful ways than our fathers and our forefathers were. One way to do this is to form or join a men's group.

A COMMUNITY OF MEN

An ongoing men's group is one of the best resources for healing the wounded male. If you aren't already in one, I suggest you join or form one. The group can serve as a community of men committed to the emotional and spiritual healing and support of one another. In your process of psychically separating from mother/Woman, it can be a very effective way of being in the world of men. Other men can provide a mirror, to reflect back to you those parts of you that you don't see, to offer perspectives you haven't considered. A mutual "fathering" takes place, a more involved, aware, and nurturing fathering than we typically got from our biological fathers. Groups offer the potential for friendships that are not focused around work, women, sports, or making money, and an opportunity to break through your sense of isolation and aloneness.

Most of us, if we open up and share our feelings at all, have learned to share our deeper feelings with women, but not with other men. While a woman can understand and empathize, only another man can accurately and truly *know* what it's like to be a man. Assuming that members are willing to take emotional risks, a group can be an excellent arena in which to open yourself emotionally to other men. Doing so tends to validate what you are feeling. In exploring and sharing emotions at increasingly deeper levels while at the same time encountering your fears of doing so, you'll find it less and less threatening to be vulnerable with other men. Openly grieving with other men, for instance, tends to lay bare the wounds, and by so doing helps heal them.

What I can personally attest to is the camaraderie that develops through sharing our grief and our joy, our triumphs and our defeats, and the depth of friendship and understanding that comes as a result of confronting our fears together. What I have seen and experienced is a profound trust that builds as men open up to each other without being put down, demeaned, ridiculed, or laughed at. Although these characteristics do not show up immediately in a men's group, or in every men's group, they can be nurtured and cultivated by a willingness on the part of the members to be conscious, open, honest, and committed.

In one instance in our men's group, Nathan came in unusually quiet. We soon discovered that his father had been hospitalized recently because of a stroke. After getting some of the details of the story—his father, age seventy-two, had the stroke when he was out working on his house—Bill asked Nathan how he was doing with all this. Nathan replied, "It's hard. I saw him in the hospital—in fact just yesterday—and it's hard to see him this way. I mean, I'm used to seeing my dad as always being

so strong, so capable. And here was this . . . old man, lying in
this hospital bed. It was strange. He couldn't speak. He couldn't
move—except for his eyes. He looked so . . . helpless. When I
looked at him he got tears in his eyes. I started crying, too.
Without saying anything we both understood that he was probably going to die soon.''

At this point Nathan broke into tears and Bill moved next
to him and put his arm on Nathan's shoulder. Everyone in the
group was quite understanding and tender with Nathan, who
was in obvious pain. We were all quite moved, and the subject
of fathers and losing fathers became the topic for the day. Many
tears were shed as each man shared something of his grief over
his own father.

FIRST STEPS: STARTING A MEN'S GROUP

These days there is an increasing number of available men's
gatherings and men's groups. Most major cities now have men's
centers cropping up. If you live in or near a major metropolitan
area, check and see if there is one locally. Through groups and
gatherings like this you can get an introduction to what it's like
being with other men in a more intense, focused way.

You will probably need to explore further, however. Although these groups can be of tremendous value, particularly in
the initial phases of work with other men, their main limitation
is that they are typically short term and lack continuity. Any
open-ended, ongoing groups have a changing membership, and
without a stable membership it's more difficult to develop and
deepen trust and intimacy to any great extent.

Another option is to look for a men's therapy group. These
are usually led by someone trained in the group process. They
can be a useful alternative when you feel the need for more
focused, intensive work. The way to go about finding one of
these is to call a number of therapists and/or agencies and let
them know you are looking for a men's group. If they them-

selves do not have one, they may be able to refer you to some-one who does.

Regardless of whatever other types of men's events, gath-erings, or groups you have been involved in, I encourage you either to start or to join an ongoing, leaderless, men's support group. I think of this type of group as a community, not because of geography but because here men are joining together for a common purpose and genuine communion. You should think in terms of being committed to this type of group for a mini-mum of two to three years. Over this period of time most people will go through a number of life changes, such as marriage, divorce, births, and deaths. By staying with the same group of men for that length of time and through these kinds of changes, you get to know each other very well.

Look Around You

Who in your life right now might be appropriate for a men's support group? Perhaps one or more friends to whom you feel close may be good candidates. Perhaps there are other men with whom you have had recent contact through business or social activities, men who struck you as having the potential for friendship and whom you feel you can trust. In particular look for men who are going through some major life passage, such as divorce or a career change. Often this is a time in a man's life when he is ripe for support and self-exploration. If you do go to a men's gathering, perhaps some of the men you meet there are potential candidates.

Don't be put off if some of the men you ask either outright reject the idea or act as if they think it's a good idea, express their interest, then drop out when it comes to a commitment. Let anyone you talk to know that it does mean a commitment; some men are simply not willing for whatever reasons to com-mit themselves to such an extent. Be selective and look for men who are motivated, trustworthy, and who you think will not only get something from a men's group but will also contribute. Even though I've been using the term "community" here to convey something of the specialness of this type of group, when talking to others about it keep it simple and call it a group. You do not need to sell the idea of the group, but simply talk about it and find out through conversation whether or not there is some interest. Far better to start with two or three others who are keenly interested than a dozen who are only marginally curious.

My first experience with any kind of men's group was ten years ago, when a group of us spent the day together on a Saturday, obviously searching for some new ways of being together as men. It was the first experience of sharing so honestly and so freely with other men. We were all quite energized by being together, but other than informal gatherings from time to time, we didn't pursue any other meetings after that one.

The group with which I have had the longest association was born of a Toastmasters club about six years ago. Toastmasters is an international organization that sponsors formatted meetings to train its members in public speaking. Because it takes some motivation to be involved in this type of club, most of the men there were already self-starters and interested in growing. There were a few of us men who, after the official Toastmasters meeting, would get together for coffee and talk. It became apparent that this informal contact was rewarding and that there was a deep yearning for man-to-man conversation. Out of these meetings came the idea that a regular meeting for men only would be extremely helpful. Many of us at the time were going through major life changes; another friend and I were both in the midst of very painful divorces, two others were contemplating changes in their work, another was having some difficulties with his ex-wife and issues regarding child custody, and still another was considering marriage. It seemed quite natural at the time to continue the momentum initiated by these informal meetings.

Set Up The Meetings

I want to stress how important it is that you be sure to invite men who are not only interested but willing to make a commitment to the group. As to numbers, the ideal group has between eight and twelve men. More than that tends to become very unwieldy.

Initially, some members may be reticent and will take a "let's wait and see" attitude. Unless the men in the group knew each other before the first meeting, there will be a period of time during which men are considering their decision whether or not they want to belong to the group. For the first couple of meetings, that sort of attitude may be fine, but after no more than four meetings, ask for a commitment from the members to ongoing participation. If someone's not interested, he will let you know. Once the commitments are declared the membership should stabilize.

Ideally, meet every week, but not less than every two weeks. Meeting once a week is clearly a considerable commitment, yet by doing so much more can happen in a shorter time. The weekly time frame also provides for greater continuity, so the group doesn't have to catch up with each member's life from meeting to meeting. As the group progresses the weekly format will also allow a more consistent reading of the evolution of the group and will encourage and expedite each individual's growth.

Although you may be taking an active leadership role in the formation and the setup of the group, the group itself should be leaderless. Leadership will emerge as it is needed, ideally with every man taking an active role in the group. Not having a designated facilitator calls on each man in the group to take personal responsibility not only for his role in the group but for the group itself.

At the first meeting of our men's group, there was a lot of enthusiasm but also a lot of uncertainty. We had no guidelines other than our collective previous experiences in men's groups. All of us expressed the desire for a greater degree of honesty and self-disclosure—and a safer atmosphere for this. Two of the members had previously attended the same men's group for a few months, and both expressed their disappointment and displeasure. As one of them put it, "All we ended up doing was talking about the women we'd had sex with and how much money we were making or going to make. I got really tired of it."

We agreed to some very simple ground rules. There would be no designated leader and we would start the meeting on time. There were no rules about what we could talk about, but we expressed a unanimous desire not to get stuck talking about women, sports, or what kind of car we drove. At that time there was little precedent for what we were trying to do, although in retrospect it's apparent that this kind of thing was happening in a few places throughout the country.

We met quite early in the morning, and as the meeting progressed, there was a palpable excitement about what we were doing. Conversation drifted quickly from one subject to the next, and by halfway through the meeting, we knew we had something special happening. We got so excited that someone suggested we keep notes and write a book. That idea took hold until someone else commented, "Isn't that just like men? Instead of just *being* together, we think we have to *do* something, like producing a book." We all had a good laugh and, just as quickly, dropped the book idea.

From these tentative beginnings, we planted the seed of something that has been and continues to be a significant source of love, support, and camaraderie for us. We had found a place where we could freely express our feelings with other men and not be harshly judged for them, which was far different than the usual men's gatherings.

Getting a group together and getting started set the groundwork for what is to come. I don't think you will have to do a lot of work after that, particularly if you emphasize from the outset the commitment and the idea that each member is to take personal responsibility for his participation. Whenever I attend any men's groups or gatherings, I always go in committed to telling the truth and taking some personal risks. These values—commitment, personal responsibility, telling the truth, and risk taking—are what will make a group grow and be alive and responsive. When these are held to and practiced, your group can collectively explore areas that you might not have thought possible, and in an atmosphere of mutual support.

Some of the areas we have explored in groups have been father-son relationships, being a father, childhood traumas, emotions, war, work and career, friendships between men, relationships with women, sex, spirituality, and environmental concerns. I recall in one group Douglas's comments during a discussion about war. He offered that he "never had to fight in a war. Shoot, I've never even been in the service. What keeps coming to me are two images from back in the late sixties. One was when I visited a friend of mine, Tony, and down the street there was a lone flag sticking out from an open porch. When I asked Tony what that was about, he said it was because there was a young man who had lived there that was killed in the war. I was struck by that image because it made the war that much more of a reality. Another was a friend of mine, one of a set of twins. His name was Dean, and he had been shot down in the war. He was a helicopter pilot or something. Well, he worked at the same gas station as I did. What I remember is how when things weren't busy he would sit by himself for the longest time, just staring into space. Nobody could really reach him. Like he was there, but wasn't there."

PASSAGES: THE LIFE CYCLE OF A MEN'S GROUP

Any group—and a group can be as few as two people—will take on a life of its own and will undergo a specific developmental sequence throughout the life of the group. Group means any cluster of people gathered together for a common purpose, and specifically here it means a men's support group. (The following ideas are adapted from the work of James Garland, Hubert Jones, and Ralph Kolodny, who described this in "A Model for Stages of Development in Social Work Groups," found in Explorations in Groupwork, edited by Sol Bernstein.)

There are five developmental stages in the life of any group: preaffiliation, affiliation, conflict, intimacy, and dissolution. Some groups go through the entire sequence; others skip conflict and intimacy and go right to dissolution. Some groups remain at the affiliation stage; others never make it past preaffiliation. Although it's possible for a group to cycle through all of these stages to some degree in a single meeting, to experience conflict and its resolution, which leads to a greater intimacy, a minimum involvement of one year is best.

Preaffiliation

This is the stage at which the various members are checking each other out to see if they want to continue spending time together. The preaffiliation process can take place before the group actually meets and can last through the first few meetings. At this stage when the group actually meets there may be a lot of testing and tentative expressions, perhaps a focus on relatively superficial topics. Men at this stage are playing it safe, in order for each member to find out where he stands with the group.

I recall one particular group that had a few men that were the core membership, with an open invitation to several other men to attend each meeting. At one meeting we ended up with twenty-two men, and had a lively discussion on father loss. A surprisingly open emotional exchange ensued, in spite of the size of the group and the newness of many of the participants. Three weeks later, we had another meeting and only eight of us came. To our surprise, very few of the men who had attended the previous meeting showed up. Although there were undoubtedly other factors, we surmised that the intensity of emotions was probably a bit scary for a lot of the newcomers.

When the group is in its earliest formative stages don't be alarmed if some members choose not to continue. There are many reasons men may not continue, since there are considerable barriers to get through not only to get to the group but to continue with it. During the preaffiliation stage the group as a whole will be doing a lot of sorting and sifting, as will each individual in the group. If it isn't right for any particular member, he will likely opt out and choose not to be affiliated.

In the initial meetings with my longest-standing men's group, there was already a strong desire on the part of most of the eight men to be affiliated. Even so, as the group went on, a couple of the men dropped out after a few meetings, and others joined. As to those who dropped out, for one it was due to the distance he had to travel and for another it was because of an overloaded schedule. After the group got well under way there were a few who came to a couple of meetings and didn't return. For some once again it was the distance they had to travel, a distance that would have interfered with regular attendance, and for others, it was that they were unwilling or unready to make the necessary commitment to be in a men's group. As I discussed earlier, a man has to confront some fears and apprehensions to sustain close friendships with other men. It took several meetings until the membership in my group stabilized, and even since then there have been other changes in membership through the life of the group.

Affiliation

The affiliation stage is a time when the group has stabilized and the members are committed to being with one another. Each member has sorted through most of his considerations and is now more invested in the group. This stage will not usually occur until you have held at least two to four meetings. With a group where membership is open and men can drift in and out without ongoing attendance, it's difficult to move past the preaffiliation stage. There can still be a lot of value in these meetings, but until the issues of commitment and stabilization are broached, the group will not likely move to the stage of affiliation. This is why a drop-in men's group has a built-in limitation. That doesn't mean it's not useful, it's just very difficult to reach the stage of genuine intimacy in a drop-in group.

Typically, the affiliation stage will last from four to twelve meetings, sometimes longer. Bonds are being formed, and a "we're all in this together" sense of fellowship is developing. In this very necessary stage men are getting to know each other better. Most members are putting on their best face, trying to be liked, trying to be receptive and tolerant of other men.

Yet simply because men *are* getting to know each other better, disagreements, judgments, and frustrations will come up for some or all of the members. You can count on it—conflict is going to be a part of *any* ongoing group. It will bubble up, sometimes staying just below the surface and remaining there, but sometimes popping forth in unexpected confrontations and surprising statements from members. If it is not honestly acknowledged and directly faced but instead remains lurking behind the masks and images of the group members, the group will falter and most likely disband. When it is acknowledged, brought out in the open, and accepted as part of the process in spite of discomfort, the group moves into the next and most difficult stage, conflict.

Conflict

Even when the members have opted to be affiliated there still may be a hesitancy to move any deeper. Once a group has become established, membership is stabilized and each man is clearly affiliated, the ground is fertile for conflict to arise openly. This will usually not happen until after at least a dozen meetings, when you have gotten to know each other better. At some point the group will grow weary of the facades that each member has erected, even the facade of silence and noninvolvement.

If conflict is not addressed and drawn out openly, the risk is that it will be acted out covertly. Members will start missing meetings or dropping out, or as a group you may end up canceling meetings. A good indication that there is some unacknowledged conflict is a feeling of restlessness or boredom while participating in the group. If the group is to move to true intimacy and be a community of men, it must learn to acknowledge, address, and work through conflict. The first step in dealing with conflict is always to acknowledge it when it is there.

In our group, conflict arose centered around one particular man who had a tendency to joke a lot and habitually give advice. Sometimes he was genuinely funny, but often his humor was coarse and distracting. This was evident to us for a few groups before we finally confronted him. Terry was talking about his new girl friend, Pauline, and some of the good feelings as well as the fears. At that point Tim made a crude joke, and the following confrontation ensued:

TERRY: Tim, I'm getting tired of your jokes all the time and your constant advice. I'm telling you guys something that's really important to me and I feel like you're not really hearing me. Sometimes what you say is funny, but a lot of times it's a pain in the ass. I'm in a situation with Pauline where I'm not feeling too steady anyway, and when you keep making a joke of it or tell me what I ought to be doing, I just want to pull back and shut up.

CHARLES: Tim, I've thought on several occasions that I get tired of your joking and interrupting but haven't said it. I was afraid you wouldn't like me or something like that. But it does distract.

TIM: You know, you're right. I do hide behind my humor. I always have. I guess it's a way to not have to deal with the pain.

JACK: What pain?

TIM: The pain of my own divorce. What you guys don't know about me is that I really hurt. I've been trying to cover it by eating a lot, but that only works very short term, and generally it just numbs me out. And the truth is, Terry, when you talk about your new relationship, I get envious, because I keep thinking, why can't I find someone like Pauline? She seems like a great gal.

Through the conflict and our willingness to address it, we achieved a new level of understanding and realness, which set the stage for greater intimacy.

It's all too human to want to avoid conflict. The initial reaction to conflict is almost always fight or flight. Many of the wounds we carry as men came as a result of conflict, especially conflict that led to violence or abrupt withdrawal by one or both parents when we were little and virtually defenseless. We are used to people hitting or leaving when there is conflict, yet there is another alternative: to accept that conflict is a part of life, and especially to accept that when you get a number of men together, there will be differences of opinion and conflict. The worst thing you can do for the group and for yourself is to avoid it altogether by pretending it isn't there. It takes courage to step into a potential fray by speaking the truth, yet it is necessary if the group is to grow and progress. Always keep in mind that the men you are with are in fundamental agreement about the purpose of being together. That purpose will provide a context for the conflict.

There are two things to keep in mind when there is conflict: Stay with it, and be willing not to be right. Staying with it means not disappearing into fight-or-flight behavior but paying attention, listening, and responding even though things may seem uncertain and chaotic for periods of times. Conflict is messy by its very nature, yet you can move with the conflict to its resolution by staying present and focused. Being willing not to be right—notice I didn't say to admit to being wrong—means dropping any righteousness or pretense to being right. Righteousness is what starts wars and makes people fight. In a group, staying right makes you hard and impenetrable, and doesn't leave any room for your vulnerability.

Intimacy

When two or more people can reveal to each other their innermost feelings and personal thoughts, you have intimacy. When you have conflict and stay with it until its conclusion, you pave the way. In fact, intimacy is naturally generated when the group is committed to taking risks and telling the truth, especially when you acknowledge and work through conflict.

Honestly expressing feelings in the safety of an ongoing group tends to empty out a lot of judgments and feelings that get in the way of genuine intimacy. When you can do this the connection you feel with the other men deepens. It may be demonstrated through words or gestures, and felt when you are crying, laughing, hugging, raging, telling stories, or doing some activity together. It's that moment when you can truly see the other person, warts and all, and accept him and feel close to him. It comes in a group when you have faced the ordeal of conflict squarely, without running or acting out, and gone through any painful feelings associated with it. What I have seen in men's groups is that intimacy creates support for further risk taking on the part of group members.

In one especially powerful group meeting we had, there were breakthroughs for all of us as a result of our willingness to share some intense and painful feelings honestly. There had already been some tears shed as the conversation gravitated to some painful childhood memories. Here's what followed:

JACK: With my mom, I was never sure—she'd always keep me guessing. Maybe it was her drinking, but she would sometimes just leave the house, without telling me or my sister where she was going! I remember one time—I must have been about six or seven—she left me in the car for what seemed like an eternity. Said she was going shopping. When she finally came back, I could smell the booze. I thought she had gotten hurt or something. I GET SO ANGRY WHEN I THINK OF THAT! *[Jack hits the cushion of the couch next to him with his fist.]* How could she do that?

BARRY: It pisses me off, too, Jack. And it must really hurt.

JACK: Yeah. *[tearfully]* I always used to think that it was my fault, that somehow I had fucked up, but she wasn't saying how.

CHARLES: Ben, what's going on with you? You got real spacey when Jack was talking.

BEN: *[He speaks very haltingly, obviously trying to hold back his tears.]* I was remembering how my dad used to put me in a closet when I was bad. And he would leave me there for a long time. I couldn't figure out always what I was doing wrong. It seemed like no matter what I did, I couldn't please him. And he would spring the closet on me and I never knew when he would do it. And it still hurts. *[At this point Ben breaks into deep heaving sobs.]*

BARRY: Come here, Ben. *[Barry sits on the floor and cradles Ben, while Ben sobs into his shoulder. The group is quiet for a long time, other than the sounds of most of the men crying.]*

Dissolution

All good things must come to an end, and at some point your group will reach the fifth and final stage, dissolution. The life cycle of the group may run for one year or for twenty. This stage may precede conflict and intimacy if the group doesn't make it over the hump of conflict. There will come a point, through membership attrition, relocation, changes in individual needs, or disinterest, when it is time to call a halt. I suspect that if the group continues to carry on the with values of truth telling and risk taking, it will be years before the group disbands. Membership may change, people will come and people will go, but the group will continue on until it's obvious that it's time to disband.

OPENING THE DOOR

Even though I've been involved in hundreds of men's groups, each time a group begins I feel both a bit nervous and excited. I get nervous because I never know quite what's going to happen, and I'm excited because I never know quite what's going to happen. Inevitably someone in the group has some situation that he is dealing with, and this is usually how the groupwork gets started. Usually there is some preliminary bantering and small talk. This may go on for several minutes, but eventually one person will bring something up that will grab the group's attention. Either that or someone speaks up and directly asks for some time and attention from the rest of the group.

Sometimes if the group is having difficulty moving past the small talk, or there is a need to open the group in a more focused way, you can use one of a couple of procedures to generate more personal dialogue and build group cohesiveness. The first is a centering meditation at the beginning of the group, and the second is a talking-stick ritual.

These procedures can be especially useful when a group is first starting out, during the phases of preaffiliation and affiliation, and can be called on again when there have been some membership changes and the group needs to restabilize. Your best bet is to experiment with these to see what's going to work for your particular group. You may find that no techniques are needed and the group moves quite easily and readily into dialogue, in which case these methods come off as more of an interference than an asset. If that becomes the case, drop the exercises and trust the group process.

Centering

Doing a centering exercise at the beginning of the group helps everyone focus on his purpose in being there and provides an informal blessing. It cuts through the small talk so the group can get down to work. When we introduced this into our men's group as a regular routine, it tended to calm some of the nervous energy that was there at the beginning of the group and provided a relaxing way to move into more personal sharing. We usually do this centering exercise about ten to fifteen minutes into the group, so there is room for greetings and some of the small talk during our initial gathering. A different person does it every week, so that it varies according to who is doing the meditation.

The following is one of my favorite centering meditations. Choose someone to read this out loud to the group. Whoever reads this can participate to the extent he can with his eyes open.

Exercise 33: Centering Together: Meditation

Close your eyes. Be aware of your breathing. Notice the rise and fall of your chest and stomach as you breathe in, then breathe out. Now take a slow, comfortable deep breath in; hold it. Now very slowly release it. Be aware of any areas of tension in your body, such as shoulders, neck, jaw, chest, stomach, buttocks, legs, or feet; as you notice these area of tension, simply breathe them out. Notice any other sensations in your body: lightness, warmth, relaxation. Notice any particular emotions that you feel.

Now be aware of the energy of the person on your left. As you shift your attention there, what do you notice? What do you sense from this person? Is he happy? Sad? Angry? Simply notice without evaluating. As you are aware of the man on your left, be aware of what goes on in your body, any sensations or emotions. Now gradually shift your attention to the person on your right. Notice his energy. What do you sense he is feeling? Can you feel his presence?

Next, shift your attention to the energy of the whole group. What do you notice as you do? What is the dominant mood of the group? Be aware of what's going on in your body as you do this.

Now return your attention to your breathing, taking another slow, comfortable deep breath. Bring your awareness into your body, into this setting. Slowly open your eyes, and when you do look around the room at the other members of the group.

Exercise 34: Centering Together: Movement

Another option for a centering exercise, either following the one above or instead of it, is a movement exercise. Everyone stand up, and move the furniture around so that each man has enough room to easily swing his arms. Put on some slow, easy to listen to music, something that will last for five to ten minutes. Once the music starts, everyone closes their eyes. Then, each participant moves his body to the music.

Stretch your legs, hips, arms, hands, and torso slowly but steadily. Feel the music in your body. Imagine the music moving you. Start slowly, then extend the stretching and the movements progressively. If there's enough room, go ahead and move your feet. Let your arms and hands express. Let your entire body express various dimensions of strength and delicacy, power and receptivity. Feel the energy in your body as you move, and enjoy the movement beyond all self-consciousness. When the music finishes, let your body slowly come to rest. When you're ready, open your eyes, and stay in your body as much as possible.

Often when a centering exercise such as one of the above is done, dialogue begins shortly afterward with very little effort.

Sometimes you may want to introduce another procedure, such as the use of the talking stick or a topic as a starting point for group discussion, as described below. Again, in your group you may have to experiment a bit to find out what is going to be the most conducive process to generate group discussion.

The Talking Stick

This is a process we've used in a couple of men's groups to stimulate dialogue as well as give each man a chance to say something. It stems from a Native American practice wherein a ceremonial wooden stick, adorned with various indigenous ornamentation and imbued with the sacred, was used by a council of men when important matters were being considered. In the meeting, whoever had the talking stick had the floor, and no one else could speak.

The procedure in your men's group could be very similar. You can create a special stick that can be used for such purpose or in a pinch, use just about anything. Once the group gets under way, someone starts by holding the stick. That man has the floor for as long as he holds the stick. It's an opportunity to share with the group whatever concerns he is dealing with at the present or to say something he needs to say to another member. For instance, if he has been feeling lonely and isolated, or is irritated with another member, this is the time to say it. It is best to be honest and speak from the heart. When he is done he passes it to someone else in the group and this continues until all have had a chance to speak. Whoever is handed the stick may choose to pass. There are to be no comments or questions when whoever holds the stick is talking. The purpose of this ground rule is to assure each person that whatever he says at this time will not be challenged, criticized, or processed. Once everyone has had a chance to have his say, put the stick aside and open the floor. From here the group may return to a particular member's comments and ask questions or respond to what someone had said during the talking-stick ceremony.

A variation of this is to do essentially the same thing without the talking stick. Without the stick you simply go around the group and let each person have from three to five minutes' time to bring everyone else up to date on what is happening in his life.

Either of these procedures gives room for everyone to say something, followed by a time for more discussion. The discussion may be quite naturally triggered by what someone said during the initial ceremony. If one of the men said something about his divorce, the conversation may easily flow into consideration of relationships and marriage. Another option, depending on the needs of the particular group, is to agree on a topic as a starting point.

STARTING POINTS

When the men involved are willing to take risks and to talk freely among themselves, there is usually little need for a thematic structure. This is particularly true when it's an ongoing group, the membership is stable, and the group has been together for several meetings. As for topics, there is plenty of material to be drawn from members' experiences, concerns, and what is brought up in the group.

There may be instances, however, when a specific topic is a useful starting point for discussion. When the group is new and still in the preaffiliation or affiliation stages, or if the group is time limited, it may be appropriate to introduce topics or questions to stimulate dialogue. These starting points are just that—questions or topics introduced to get things rolling. Once the dialogue is under way, there is typically no need to force or direct it, even if it does get off the topic. While certainly not exhaustive, below are a few topics and questions that can be useful in opening things up. These are the kinds of topics and questions that have been raised and dealt with in other men's groups and workshops.

One effective way to use these is to bring this list to one of the first meetings and agree on one of the topics and/or one of the questions for the following meeting. You can repeat this procedure as long as it is necessary. Another method is to write out a few of the topics/questions on separate sheets of paper, put these into a hat or bowl, and choose one. That becomes the topic of that particular group. You can also do something similar by having each member write a question or area of concern on a small sheet of paper, put those into a hat, draw them, and vote on the one that is appealing to the majority of men.

I trust that these will be helpful starting points for any group, if needed. Again, once the group has stabilized, topics will tend to be spontaneously generated from the group process. However, if the group bogs down, some of these can be introduced to spark a discussion.

Manhood

What is the hardest thing about being a man? The easiest?

What do you like best about your manhood?

Who do you think has it easier, men or women, and why?

Who are the men in your life you most admire? What is it about these men that you like?

Who has been a significant mentor in the past? How did he affect you?

Who are your mentors presently? What do you learn from them?

What are some of the ways you were initiated into manhood? How have these experiences affected you today?

Have you ever been hurt by a man? Who was it? What happened? How has this affected you still today?

Whom do you trust more, women or men? Why?

Who is your closest male friend? What do you like about him? How do you express your friendship?

Fathers

What kind of relationship did you have with your father? If he is still alive, what is that relationship like now?

What do you want your father to know about you that he doesn't know? What do you want to know about him? What do you want to say to him before he dies?

What's the thing you like the least about your father? What do you like the most?

In your childhood, what incidents with your father stand out the most? How were you as a child with him? When were the happiest times? The unhappiest?

In what ways are you like your father? How are you different?

If you are not yet a father, would you like to be? Why?

If you are a father, what do you want your children to learn from you? How have you affected them so far? How do you want to change your fathering, if at all?

Emotions

What is the hardest feeling for you to express? What gets in the way?

Traditionally, it has been harder for men to express their feelings than women. Why do you suppose that is true? Has it been true for you? If so, would you like to change?

How do you deal with your anger or rage? Have you been hurt by anger? How?

Of what are you most afraid? How do you deal with that fear? Has fear ever been your ally?

What is one of the saddest moments in your life?

What is one of the happiest times you've ever experienced?

Do you think that men feel differently than women? If so, how?

What are the major losses in your life? Have you grieved them? When you talk about them do you feel that you are finished grieving or are there still some feelings?

Work And Money

What do you like best about the work you do? The least?

If you could be doing any job that you wanted without concern for money or status, what would you be doing? What gets in the way of your doing this?

What attitudes about work do you carry with you from your father or mother? What did you learn about money from them?

If you learned that you have only one year to live, that you would not be limited in what you could physically do until the last couple of weeks, what would you do differently, if anything?

How do you want to be remembered when you die? What achievements, accomplishments are you especially proud of?

What does it mean to be successful? When have you felt that way? How do you measure success?

Have you ever failed or felt like a failure? What was that like?

Do you consider yourself ambitious? If so, what's the driving
   force behind your ambition? If not, why not?

Why do you work? What are your primary motivators?

How much money do you make? What's your net worth? Why
   is it so hard to talk about this with other men?

Sex And Love

How did you first learn about sex? What were some of the mis-
   conceptions you had?

What attitudes did you learn from your father about sex? From
   your mother?

How old were you when you started masturbating? How did you
   feel about it?

How do you feel about your penis? Are you satisfied with your
   size? What other names do you have for your penis?

Have you ever been impotent? How did you feel about it?

How have your attitudes about sex and love changed over the
   years?

What was your first sexual experience like? Was it with someone you loved?

How do you feel about commitment in a relationship?

Have you ever felt sexual toward another man? If so, how did
   you deal with it?

What does it take to be intimate with someone else? Is sex
   always a part of intimacy? When do you feel the most intimate with a woman? A man?

Under what conditions is sex best for you? With someone you
   are in a relationship with? With someone you've picked up?
   A friend?

What qualities do you look for in a woman? Are they different
   in someone you want to have sex with as opposed to someone with whom you want to be in a committed relationship?

Spirituality

What sort of religious practices did your parents have? How did religion influence your earlier upbringing?

What value, if any, do you find in religion today?

What are the differences in religion and spirituality?

Do you believe in God or a Higher Power? How do you see Him/Her?

How have your spiritual beliefs and practices changed over the years?

What do you believe happens after death?

In a men's group you will be able to meet many of the needs that most of us have pushed aside or altogether denied, particularly the need to be close and real with other men. A men's group has a sort of tribal quality to it. Whatever the form of the group or of any other types of relationships with other men, I encourage you to maintain and nurture those relationships. Being involved with a community of men is an absolutely critical part of your healing.

The journey of healing your woundedness is a major project, perhaps the biggest and at times most challenging one you will ever have undertaken. It will require your courage, your trust, and your dedication, as well as a willingness to seek support from others. By doing what we need to do to heal our wounds, we recover a deeper, instinctual part of our masculine nature that has been buried under the rubble of denial for generations. We recover our ability to feel passionate and alive, from the inside out, not via some external means of stimulation like work, sex, or a relationship. It is through this healing process that we discover what it means to be a vulnerable warrior, a mature man in the truest sense of the word. And as we heal our wounds, an amazing thing begins to happen. We heal our relationships with others around us, and with our precious planet earth. Is there any other path to take?

Suggested Readings

Abbott, Franklin, ed., *New Men, New Minds: Breaking Male Tradition.* Freedom, Calif.: The Crossing Press, 1987.

Bly, Robert. *Iron John: A Book about Men.* Reading, Mass.: Addison-Wesley Publishing Company, Inc., 1990.

Farrell, Warren. *Why Men Are the Way They Are.* New York: McGraw-Hill, 1986.

Gilmore, David D. *Manhood in the Making: Cultural Concepts of Masculinity.* London: Yale University Press, 1990.

Johnson, Robert. *He: Understanding Masculine Psychology.* rev. ed. New York: Harper & Row, 1989.

Keen, Sam. *Fire in the Belly: On Being a Man.* New York: Bantam Books, 1991.

Lawlor, Robert. *Earth Honoring: The New Male Sexuality.* Rochester, Vt.: Park Street Press, 1989.

Lee, John. *The Flying Boy: Healing the Wounded Man.* Deerfield Beach, Fla.: Health Communications, Inc., 1987.

Masters, Robert Augustus. *The Way of the Lover: The Awakening & Embodiment of the Full Human.* Vancouver, B.C.: Xanthyros Foundation, 1988.

Millman, Dan. *Way of the Peaceful Warrior: A Book that Changes Lives.* Tiburon, Calif.: H. J. Kramer, Inc., 1984.

Nelson, James B. *The Intimate Connection: Male Sexuality, Masculine Spirituality*. Philadelphia: The Westminster Press, 1988.

Osherson, Sam. *Finding Our Fathers: The Unfinished Business of Manhood*. New York: The Free Press, 1986.

Sanford, John A., and Lough, George. *What Men Are Like: The Psychology of Men, for Men and the Women Who Live With Them*. New York: Paulist Press, 1988.

ABOUT THE AUTHOR

Steven Farmer is an international speaker, bestselling author, and psycho-therapist with a private practice in Irvine, California, where he specializes in men's issue, codependency and Adult Child issues.